NORTH CAROLINA

'Round the Mountains

GUIDE BOOK

The most comprehensive guide book
of the Western North Carolina mountains
by
Ruth Camblos and Virginia Winger

D1414117

Copyright © 1981 by Ruth Cam~
Fourth Edition
ISBN: 0-9602706-3-9

Library of Congress Catalog Card number: 81-52951

Printed by
GROVES PRINTING COMPANY
Asheville, N. C.

ASHEVILLE AREA CHAMBER OF COMMERCE

OFFICE OF THE EXECUTIVE VICE PRESIDENT

Dear Friends:

All the goals and objectives of the Asheville Area Chamber of Commerce are directed toward improving the quality of life in our community. This includes making available as much information as possible for residents and visitors alike.

Of particular informative value is a locally published book, Round the Mountains. It is a very readable, enjoyable guidebook about the Southern Appalachian Highlands. You will find maps, illustrations and descriptive information about outstanding historical sites, special events and principle sightseeing and tourist attractions in this area. It includes shopping information, mountain crafts, art, jewelry-making, outlets and other area specialties, as well as a list of restaurants and take-home food shops.

We are happy to endorse this book and hope you will use it to enhance the enjoyment of your vacation.

Sincerely,

James E. Ellis

James E. Ellis, CCE

JEE/pdr

Post Office Box 1011 ● 151 Haywood Street ● Asheville, North Carolina 28802 ● 704/258-5200

To order single copies: Send name and address with check for $6.50 payable to **Round The Mountains.** Price includes postage and handling. (N. C. residents add 20¢ sales tax) write: **Round The Mountains,** P. O. Box 15424, Asheville, NC 28813.

Western North Carolina
Travel & Promotion Association, Inc.

July, 1981

Greetings to Travel Enthusiasts:

Western North Carolina is a variety vacationland which is yours
to discover. The high mountain peaks and the clear, cool streams
invite you to share the scenic beauty of our land and our people.
Whatever your tastes, there are places to go and things to do for
everyone.

The topics in <u>Round the Mountains Guide Book</u> are designed to make
travelers aware of the many places and events in the southern
mountain region of North Carolina. The guide book is one of the
most resourceful services to residents and visitors alike. It is
a complete and easy to read guide which lists lodging and resort
information, restaurants, and visitor attractions. For the
shopping enthusiast, outlets and specialty shops are listed.
Through the guide book, discover the historic sites, arts, and
crafts which are preserved in our town and cities.

We hope you will find <u>Round the Mountains Guide Book</u> useful
during your stay in Western North Carolina. We invite you to
come and discover the natural beauty of our land and enjoy our
mountain hospitality.

Sincerely,

Ronald G. Hill, President
Western North Carolina
Travel & Promotion Association, Inc.

Courthouse • Murphy, NC 28906 • 704 — 837-5527

TABLE OF CONTENTS

APPROXIMATE MILES FROM ASHEVILLE

TO	MILES	TO	MILES
Bakersville	69	Hot Springs	40
Balsam	39	**Knoxville**	120
Banner Elk (via Marion)	86	Lake Junaluska	28
(via Parkway)	96	Lake Lure	26
Barnardsville	16	Lake Toxaway	53
Bat Cave	21	Linville	69
Black Mountain	19	Little Switzerland	51
Blowing Rock	88	Maggie Valley	36
Boone	100	Marion	31
Brasstown	102	Marshall	22
Brevard	28	Mars Hill	18
Bryson City	63	Montreat	17
Burnsville	40	Mt. Mitchell	36
Canton	18	Murphy	108
Cashiers	64	Nantahala	81
Cherokee	49	Old Fort	23
Chimney Rock	24	Pisgah Forest	32
Crossnore	65	Ridgecrest	16
Cullowhee	60	Roan Mountain	88
Dillsboro	51	Robbinsville	95
Flat Rock	25	Rosman	42
Fletcher	18	Rutherfordton	46
Fontana	114	Saluda	32
Franklin	69	Spruce Pine (via 19E)	56
Gastonia	105	(via Parkway)	66
Grandfather Mountain	81	Swannanoa	8
Hendersonville	23	Sylva	49
Hickory	74	Tryon	40
High Hampton	64	Waynesville	40
Highlands	74	Weaverville	18

V

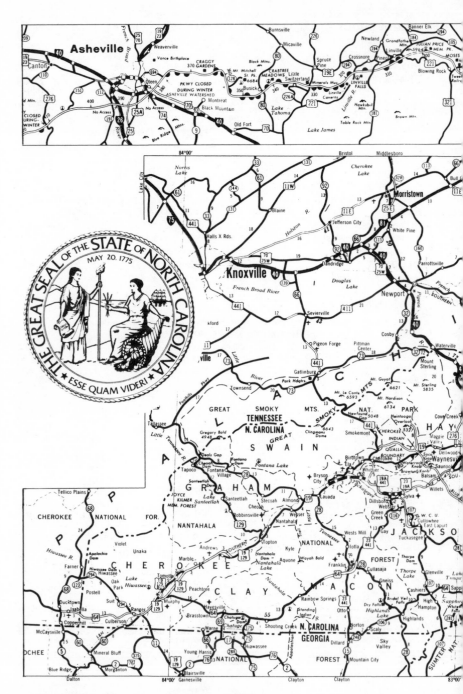

Map: N.C. Department of Transportation

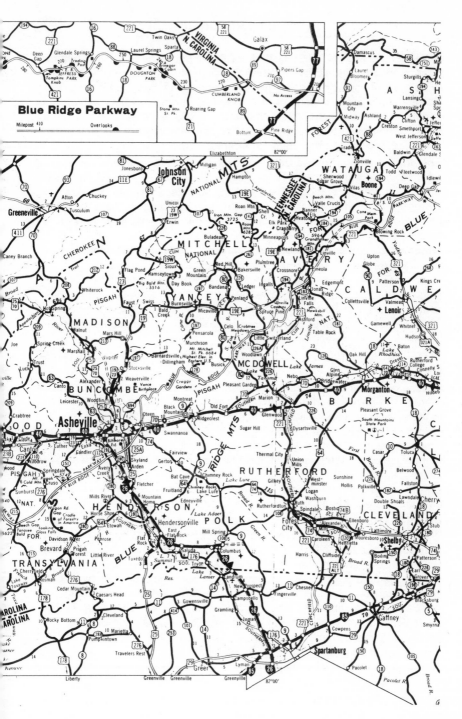

Blue Ridge Parkway

Milepost 410 ———— Overlooks ————

ABOUT THIS BOOK

ROUND THE MOUNTAINS GUIDE BOOK is compiled to provide helpful information about the Western North Carolina Mountains, and it continues to be the most comprehensive guide book covering the vacation area. The Guide details information about sightseeing, lodging, resorts, restaurants, shops, entertainment, historic buildings, crafts, antiques, sports, gem mining, festivals, music, dancing, theater, amusement parks, outlet shopping and many other items of interest to the vacationer.

The fourth edition of **ROUND THE MOUNTAINS** contains extensive information about our national forests, the Blue Ridge Parkway, the Great Smoky Mountains National Park and the Appalachian Trail. Because of increased interest in hiking, backpacking and camping, we have included campgrounds and recreational opportunities in these national parks and forests.

Elevation is expressed in feet and distance is indicated by miles.

County information with historical sketches are additions to the Guide. Popular country inns, resorts, restaurants, shops and sightseeing have been arranged by county for easier reference. To obtain more information about accommodations, request the Western North Carolina Lodging Guide from the Chamber of Commerce in Asheville or the county you plan to visit.

OUTLETS are grouped in the back of the book for the reader's convenience.

In our eighth year as publishers and compilers, we are indebted to our many friends who advise and help us in collecting valuable information. We wish to thank them all, especially the collective Chambers of Commerce and the officials of the Blue Ridge Parkway, the U. S. Forest Service and the Great Smoky Mountains National Park. Credit lines are given to those who have written specific sketches. Photographs are credited as they appear. We send special thanks to Miss Ora Blackmun, author of *Western North Carolina Its Mountains and Its People to 1880,* who advised us on historical data and to Peggy Guthrie for her contribution to the material about hiking.

ROUND THE MOUNTAINS GUIDEBOOK has been endorsed by the Western North Carolina Travel and Promotion Association, Inc., the Asheville Chamber of Commerce, the Asheville Tourism Association, the Biltmore Company and the Blue Ridge Parkway. Their endorsements and encouragement of our work have helped us establish our objectives. Our special thanks also extend to Hugh Morton, of Grandfather Mountain, for our cover photographs. We sincerely hope that **ROUND THE MOUNTAINS GUIDEBOOK** will entertain and inform you, as well as entice you to visit beautiful Western North Carolina.

Ruth Camblos and Virginia Winger, Publishers
NORTH CAROLINA ROUND THE MOUNTAINS GUIDEBOOK
P. O. Box 15424
Asheville, NC 28813

THE WESTERN NORTH CAROLINA MOUNTAINS

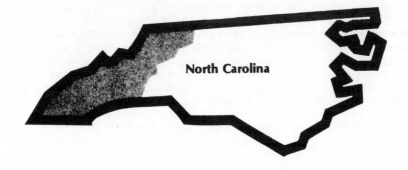

North Carolina

GEOGRAHICAL SKETCH

The Appalachian Mountains extend from Newfoundland, the Gaspe Peninsula and New Brunswick in Canada 1,200 miles into central Alabama. Two parts of the system are the Blue Ridge and Great Smoky Mountain ranges. The Blue Ridge is the eastern rim of an elevated land mass that varies in width from 15 to 70 miles. Elevations average from 1500 to 2500 feet. However, numerous peaks are over 5000 and 6000 feet. Mount Mitchell in North Carolina is the highest peak in the United States east of the Mississippi River Basin. Its elevation is 6684 feet. Clingman's Dome in the Great Smoky Mountains National Park is 6642 feet. The Blue Ridge is the older range and the watershed. It's rivers cut deep channels and flow westward to the Cumberland and Tennessee Rivers toward the Ohio River. Granites and Paleozoic sediments are the rock divisions in the Applachian belt. Many valuable stones including gems as well as mica and talc are mined in the southern region. Extensive timber forests produce hardwoods and white and yellow pine. A soft blue haze clings to the mountains and gives the Blue Ridge its name.

THE PEOPLE

The year 1750 marked the beginning of the great Southern migration. Scotch-Irish and German Settlers by the thousands traveled along "the great Philadelphia Wagon Road" into North Carolina. The main stream flowed through Pennsylvania, the valley of Virginia, and the Piedmont of the two Carolinas.

Pioneers of the North Carolina Piedmont represented religious reform groups. Some German Lutherans settled in the Yadkin Valley, but the largest reform group was made up of Scotch-Irish Presbyterians. These Scotch-Irish had begun their migration to America in the early 1700's. Originally from Ulster, in Northern Ireland, they were descendants of Protestant Scottish Lowlanders deported by James I to Northern Ireland around 1610. Known in Europe as Ulstermen, they were called Scotch-Irish in America.

These people became our frontiersmen. On the Colonial frontier were found English, Irish, and French Huguenots, but the Scotch-Irish and Germans predominated in Western expansion. Border people by tradition, the Scotch-Irish were adept at border wars. Patriotic and fearless in their new country, they were effective in the French and Indian War and in the Revolutionary War. It has been estimated that by 1790 a quarter of a million Americans had Scotch-Irish ancestry.

When mountain land became available after the Revolution, these same settlers moved into Western North Carolina, bringing their independence, initiative, and many skills to create a new life in the wilderness. They were hardy, energetic outdoor people, willing to pay with hard labor the price for political and religious freedom.

French Broad River   Photo by - Jack R. Gwennap

FRENCH BROAD RIVER. Prior to 1763 when the land drained by this river was claimed by the French, hunters and traders called this the Broad River for its wide adjacent lowlands. They soon discovered, however, that there was another "Broad River" in English territory just east of the Blue Ridge so they started referring to this as the "French" Broad River.. *U.S. Dept. of Interior, National Park Service.*

THE CRAFT STORY

Great wealth is represented in the many skills and talents unique to these mountains. Artisans of pottery, wood-carving and weaving are continuing lifetime occupations handed down through many generations. In the Appalachians this heritage has lived because several forces have been at work to protect it.

Rural settlement schools placed in remote areas by religious and fraternal organizations taught useful skills to mountain children. Some of the finest craft schools in the nation teach and train students from all over the world in the arts of weaving, pottery, wood carving, glass-blowing and jewelry making. Outstanding craft schools in this region: Penland School, Penland, N.C. (near Spruce Pine), The John C. Campbell Folk School, Brasstown, N.C. (near Murphy), and Arrowmont, Gatlinburg, Tenn. Guilds, federal agencies and others have aided in marketing the products. The Southern Highland Handicraft Guild, Asheville, N.C. and the Blue Ridge Hearth-Side Crafts Association, Inc., Sugar Grove, N.C. (near Boone) have contributed greatly. Some exceptional craftsmen choose to remain independent from the guilds, and we salute them also. Artisans appear with their work at the frequent summer and fall craft festivals. Visit them and select a craft piece as you would any work of art — because it appeals to your eye. A note on buying pottery: Ceramics describes any ware made of baked clay. Do not confuse with mold-poured "greenware." Thrown or handbuilt pottery is the kind you will want to purchase. Earthenware, stoneware and porcelain are all ceramics. Earthenware is fired at low temperatures and is desirable for oven use; however, it must be well glazed on the inside. Stoneware is fired at much higher temperature and may be used for cooking. It is sturdier and non-porous. Porcelain is fired at an even higher temperature than stoneware and is made from fine white material called "china clay" along with some materials used in glass making. Its beauty shows when thinly formed, appearing transluscent. Fragile.

MOUNTAIN MUSIC AND DANCING

An important part of our culture in Western North Carolina is the heritage preserved in mountain music and dancing. Through these two forms of self-expression much of the colorful mountain history lies today. Traditional bands have no amplified instruments. A typical band consists of a flat-top guitar, a hoe-down fiddle, a 5-string banjo, a double bass and often a mandolin and/or a dobro. Our "Highland minstrels" sing true-to-life songs, comedy songs and spirituals. The standard repertoire would contain instrumental tunes played at lightning speed, old and new ballads and often intricate harmonies performed in the old revival style of southern spirituals.

Today there are many organized bands and dance teams performing in the traditional folk styles. Pickin' singin' and dancin' can be found in several spots in Western North Carolina.

-by Mark Pruett

TROUT FISHING IN WESTERN NORTH CAROLINA

The mountain trout species in North Carolina are brook trout, brown trout and rainbow trout. Certain waters in the western part of the state are designated as public mountain trout waters. Of these, some are further designated as native trout waters and trophy trout waters with the remainder being classified as general trout waters. Fishing in designated public mountain trout waters is limited to hook and line only, with only one line per person. In native trout waters only single-hook artificial lures are permitted. Only single-hook artificial flies may be used on the four trophy trout waters. General and native waters are open from April through February , and trophy waters are open year round. A few of the better trout waters are described below:

DAVIDSON RIVER. General water from the mouth of Avery's Creek downstream; native water from the mouth of Avery's Creek upstream. *From Brevard take NC 276, which follows the river for five miles.*

SOUTH MILLS RIVER. Trophy water from the National Forest boundary upstream for about seven miles to Cantrell Creek, beyond which native regulations apply. *From Brevard take NC 280 to Forest Service Road 297 at the Transylvania/Henderson County line.*

ROCKY BROAD RIVER. General water and a tributary to Lake Lure. *From Asheville take US 74 to Bat Cave then east on US 64/74, which closely parallels the river to the downstream limit of public fishing.*

NANTAHALA RIVER. From the bridge at the Standing Indian Campground in Nantahala National Forest upstream the river is native water; from the bridge downstream to the National Forest boundary, the river is trophy water. *Take US 64 west from Franklin to Wallace Gap, then the Forest Service Road to the campground.* Outside the National Forest general fishing regulations apply. *Take US 64 west from Franklin through Wallace Gap to Rainbow Springs, then Forest Service Road about five miles to Roaring Fork Bridge.* A quarter-mile trail downstream leads to the upper limit of public fishing.

SOUTH TOE RIVER. Native waters in the Mount Mitchell Wildlife Management Area. *From Busick in Yancey County take NC 80 less than a mile; turn left on Forest Service Road 472, which follows the river much of the way and comes out on the Blue Ridge Parkway at Deep Gap.*

CANE RIVER. General waters. *From Burnsville in Yancey County take US 19-E west to State Road 1139, then right on NC 197 to the bridge at Bowlens Creek. About eight miles of fishing upstream to Pensacola.*
Fishing is popular in the Great Smoky Mountains National park, where the season is from April 15 - October 15. Special regulations apply, and a copy of them can be obtained at any ranger station in the Park or from The Superintendent, GSMNP, Gatlinburg, TN. 37738.

Certain streams on the Cherokee Indian Reservation are open for public fishing for a small daily fee from the first Saturday in April until October 31. About thirty miles of streams and three ponds are stocked weekly,and most of the waters are easily accessible.

There are many other trout streams in the North Carolina mountains, and most of them have been described in detail in TROUT FISHING WATERS OF NORTH CAROLINA, a $4.85 paperback that gives directions to each water as well as a popularity rating for each stream. For a copy of it, or a copy of the current fishing regulations or a brochure describing trout fishing on the Cherokee Indian Resevation, write the Plumlea Angler, Route 3, Box 123, Fletcher, NC 28732.

Marshall Roberts

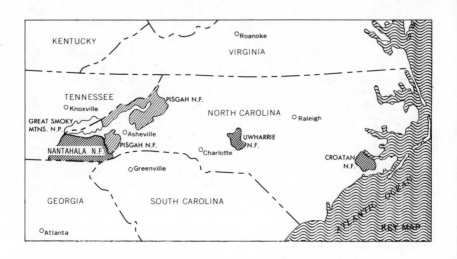

WESTERN NORTH CAROLINA NATIONAL PARKS & FORESTS
ADMINISTERED BY:

GREAT SMOKY MOUNTAINS NATIONAL PARK	517,659 acres N.C. and Tennessee	National Park Service U.S. Dept. of the Interior
APPALACHIAN TRAIL	282.02 miles in N.C.	Appalachian Trail Conference;U.S. Dept. of the Interior; U.S. Dept of Agriculture
NANTAHALA and PISGAH NATIONAL FOREST	959,388 acres In N.C.	Forest Service U.S. Dept. of Agriculture
BLUE RIDGE PARKWAY	470 miles N.C. & Virginia	National Park Service U.S. Dept of the Interior.

INTRODUCTION

The opportunity to see and enjoy the beauty of the unspoiled wilderness of the Southern Appalachian Mountains is readily available for all visitors to Western North Carolina. The **Great Smoky Mountains National Park** is one of the most accessible and frequently visited National Parks in the United States. The **Nantahala** and **Pisgah National Forests** contain 959,388 acres in 18 counties in Western North Carolina. There are three wilderness areas within the National Forests: **Joyce Kilmer-Slickrock Wilderness, Shining Rock** and **Linville Gorge Wilderness** areas. The **Appalachian Trail** beckons the hiker.

The **Blue Ridge Parkway** makes its way for 253 miles through the North Carolina mountains, affording the automobile traveler spectacular scenery.

To fully appreciate this magnificent land, one should leave the main highways and venture forth to discover the essence and grandeur of the mountains.

This section of **Round the Mountains** is designed to help you do just that. In **Our Southern Highlanders** Horace Kephart quotes naturalist John Muir as saying "our forests, 'however slighted by man, must have been a great delight to God; for they were the best he ever planted'." You will surely agree.

1

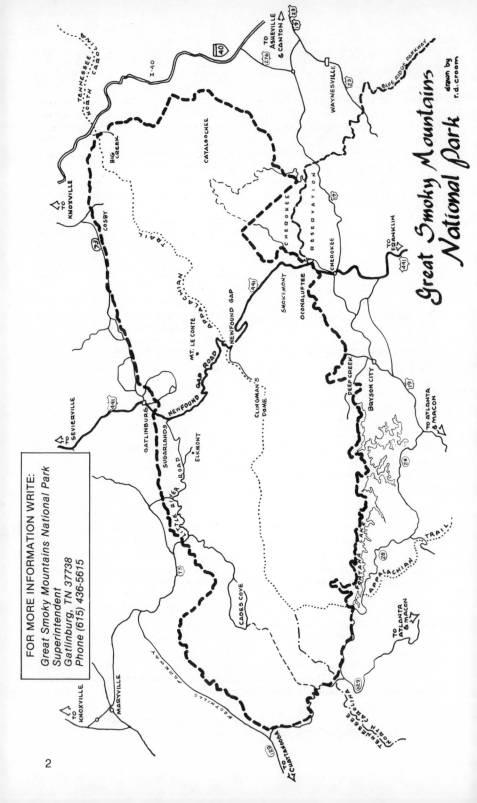

Great Smoky Mountains
National Park

drawn by
r.d. croom

FOR MORE INFORMATION WRITE:
Great Smoky Mountains National Park
Superintendent
Gatlinburg, TN 37738
Phone (615) 436-5615

2

GREAT SMOKY MOUNTAINS NATIONAL PARK

The Great Smokies mountain range runs east and west for 70 miles along the North Carolina-Tennessee border. Containing over a half million acres, it is the most massive mountain range in the eastern United States. There are 16 peaks over 6,000 feet in elevation. Geologists have determined that the Smokies, as part of the southern Appalachians, are the oldest mountains in the U.S., and some of the oldest in the world. Formed 125 million years before the Rockies, they are older still than the Alps and Himalayas.

With its virtually unspoiled forests, the Smokies are noted as a Wilderness Sanctuary that preserves one of the finest examples of deciduous forests in the world. Conifer forests are like those in Central Canada. Rich soil and moisture have produced a world renowned variety of flora with more than 1400 kinds of flowering plants. There is abundant wild life-small animals and birds, white tailed deer, and the Park's famous residents, approximately 400 to 600 Black Bears.

Millions of years of life preceded the recorded history of the Great Smokies. Peopled by Cherokees and then by hardy pioneers in the 1700's, the Smokies remained relatively unchanged, unknown and unchartered until the early 1900's when the logging industry moved in and began to clear cut entire sections. Through the conservation efforts of men like Arno B. Cammerer and Horace Kephart, Congress in 1926 passed a bill to create the Great Smoky Mountains National Park. No funds were alloted for land purchase; for some time land acquisition was left to private citizens, communities and the states of North Carolina and Tennessee. By 1934 a grant from John D. Rockefeller, Jr. and some federal funding made it possible for the area to reach full National Park status.

Today the Great Smoky Mountains National Park is one of the most popular Parks in the country, with millions of visitors each year. The Newfound Gap road from Cherokee to Gatlinburg goes through the center of the Park and affords the traveler spectacular views. This road is generally congested during the summer and fall months. Camping in the Park varies from developed areas accessible by car to primitive back-country campsites accessible only on foot. Over 800 miles of horse and foot trails interlace the Park. About 70 miles of the Appalachian Trail follows the North Carolina-Tennessee line.

The visitor interested in learning more about the Park is referred to the Sierra Club's *Hiker's Guide to the Smokies*, a book rich in history and description of wildlife, plants and trees.

SPECIAL INFORMATION:

SUGARLANDS VISTIOR CENTER: *U.S. 441 near Gatlinburg, Tennessee, entrance to the Park.* Visitor Center and Park Headquarters. Open daily until 7:30 p.m. during summer. Daily activities: Field trips. Illustrated lectures on flora, fauna, park history.
OCONALUFTEE VISITOR CENTER: *U.S. 441 and Blue Ridge Parkway terminus near Cherokee, N.C.* Information, exhibits, publications. Open daily. Other activities: **PIONEER FARMSTEAD.** A 1900's re-created mountain farm. Active history demonstrations. **MINGUS MILL:** Open daily. Watch the miller grind corn. Cornmeal available.

SPECIAL INFORMATION

CADES COVE VISITOR CENTER: *Little River Road off Newfound Gap Road at Sugarlands.* Open daily 9-5. Information and exhibits on pioneer life. Cades Cove is an 11 mile loop road leading past fields, churches and pioneer homesteads. **Cable Mill:** Water powered grist mill. Daily demonstrations. Cades Cove can also be reached through the Townsend entrance to the Park. *Hwy. 73.*

SELF-GUIDING NATURE TRAILS: Balsam Mountain, Spruce-Fir, Sugarlands Cove Hardwoods, Cosby, Noah "Bud" Ogle, Mids Branch, Pine-Oak, Smokemont. All are 1 mile or less. Check a Park map for general location.

ANNUAL SPRING WILDFLOWER PILGRIMAGE: *Usually the last full weekend in April. Pilgrimage program features guided tours.*

CLINGMAN'S DOME: *Off U.S. 441. Highest peak (6,642) and lookout tower.*

NEWFOUND GAP: *Elevation: 5,048. Crest of the trans-mountain highway between Cherokee, N.C. and Gatlinburg, Tenn. Clingman's Dome route joins U.S. 441 at this point.*

MT. LE CONTE: *Elevation: 6,593. Five Trails to Mt. Le Conte.*

BLUE RIDGE PARKWAY: *470 mile scenic mountain top road. Entrance Great Smoky Mountains Parkway boundary ½ mile below Oconaluftee Visitor Center. Near Cherokee, N.C.*

CAMPING: Seven developed campgrounds and three primitive campgrounds are located in the Park.

CADES COVE, SMOKEMONT and ELKMONT are developed campgrounds with reservation system May 1 - Nov. 1. Reservations by mail **at this address only:** *Ticketron Reservation Office, P.O. Box 1715, San Francisco, Ca. 94126.* Walk-in reservations can be made at above camp grounds or Sugarland and Oconaluftee Visitor Center. All other camp grounds in the Park operate on a first-come, first-served basis: Cosby, Deep Creek, Look Rock, Abrams Creek, Big Creek, Cataloochee and Balsam Mountain. Back country overnight camping in the Smokies requires a permit. For information call: *GSMNP (615) 436-5615 or write: GSMNP, Gatlinburg, TN, 37738.*

CADES COVE CAMPGROUND: Only store in the National Park. Picnic supplies.

HORSEBACK RIDING: Available April through October. Five riding stables in the Park.

ACCOMMODATIONS:

LE CONTE LODGE: *Top of Mt. Le Conte. Open late March to early November.* Secluded retreat. Meals and lodging. Accessible only by foot or horse trail. Five trails. (take lunch). For rates and reservations: *Le Conte Lodge, P.O. Box 350, Gatlinburg, Tn. 37738. Phone (615) 436-4473.*

WONDERLAND CLUB HOTEL: *Open late May through late October.* Rustic, semi-secluded, early 1900's hotel. Lodging and meals. Accessible by car, 7½ miles west of Gatlinburg, Tn., via Little River Road and Elkmont Road. For rates and information: *Wonderland Club Hotel, Rt. 2, Gatlinburg, Tn. 37738. Phone (615) 436-5490.*

4

THE APPALACHIAN TRAIL

For detailed information write:
The Appalachian Trail Conference
P.O. Box 236
Harper's Ferry, West Virginia, 25425

The Appalachian Trail is a marked hiking trail recommended for experienced hikers. It winds for 2,015 miles through the great Appalachian Mountain System from Mount Katahdin, Maine, to Springer Mountain, Georgia. A National Scenic Trail, it crosses into N.C. near Damascus, Va. The trail generally follows the Tennessee-North Carolina border through the Cherokee and Pisgah National Forests continuing for 68 miles through the Great Smoky Montains National Park and south through the Nantahala National Forest into Georgia.

The 282 mile section of the A.T. through North Carolina is considered by many to be the most rugged of its 2,015 mile course from Maine to Georgia. Hikers will cross many peaks over 5000 feet. Parts of the A.T. in North Carolina are extremely congested. Because of over-crowding it is necessary to ration overnight use of the 70 miles of the A.T. within the Great Smoky Mountains National Park. Shelters are limited according to the number of bunks.

Other sections of the A.T. in Pisgah and Nantahala National Forests are less crowded and do not require permits for overnight use.

The Appalachian Trail is constructed for travel on foot. It is not suited for bicycle or horse travel generally and motor vehicles are prohibited.

The Forest Service advises that the Trail offers the hiker a challenge that should not be underestimated, requiring advance planning and physical fitness.

Trail markers direct the hiker. Miles of walking are rewarded with magnificent scenery and the opportunity to observe Appalachian animals and plants in their natural setting.

Northeast of the Great Smokies the A.T. goes through the town of Hot Springs in Madison County, N.C. Crossing the bridge over the French Broad River, the A.T. signs take the hiker right down Main Street. Bed, bath and restaurants are available. Ask for the "Trailburger." We recommend:

HOT SPRINGS HIKERS HOSTEL. *US 25-70. (704) 622-3248.* Sixth year of operation by the Jesuits of the Maryland province who have been located in Madison County since 1927. Accommodatins for about 35 hikers or students. On Appalachian trail. On grounds are the Jesuit Residence and Redeemer Catholic Chapel. Open to public. Call for reservations. Ecumenical retreats.

PISGAH AND NANTAHALA NATIONAL FORESTS

In Western North Carolina the Pisgah and Nantahala National Forests cover approximately one million acres. Within the National Forests are three Wilderness Areas: *Shining Rock, Linville Gorge and Joyce Kilmer-Slickrock Wilderness.* Almost all of this land is within one hundred miles of Asheville. Almost half is within fifty miles of the city.

Dozens of camping and picnicking areas and hundreds of miles of hiking trails and fishing streams are within an easy days drive of any Western North Carolina town. Some of the excellent National Forest campgrounds are *Standing Indian near Franklin, Black Mountain near Mount Mitchell, Lake Powhatan near Asheville and Rocky Bluff south of Hot Springs.*

RECREATION AREAS - include developed and primitive camping sites, picnicking areas and wilderness areas. There are 30 Recreation Areas in Pisgah National Forest. A fee is now charged to use some Federal Recreation Areas including some in National Forests.

The wide variety of campgrounds range in the degree of comfort to the camper. There are developed campgrounds with comfort stations and primitive campgrounds for the tent camper. Most developed campgrounds can accommodate 22' Recreational Vehicles.

Primitive camping without permit is allowed anywhere in the National Forests unless posted otherwise. Permits are required for entrance to **Linville Gorge** and **Shining Rock Wilderness** and can be obtained at District Ranger Stations that adminster these areas.

Hunting and fishing are allowed under State of North Carolina regulations. Contact: *N.C. Wildlife Commission for information.*

PISGAH NATIONAL FOREST

The nucleus of Pisgah National Forest consisted of approximately a hundred thousand acres of mountain land owned by George Vanderbilt. After his untimely death in 1914, it was sold to the National Forest Reservation Commission. Mrs. Vanderbilt specified that the area should be embraced in a national forest to be known as the Pisgah National Forest. In **Birth of Forestry in America** Carl Alwin Schenck said, "It was characteristic of her to want the forestry dreams of her husband and the beautiful mountain country in which they had taken root saved, not merely as an object lesson, but also for the use and enjoyment of the American public."

Presently containing 490,914 acres of land in twelve Western North Carolina counties, the Pisgah National Forest is administered by the Forest Service of the U.S. Dept of Agriculture. In addition to recreational opportunities, the Forest supplies water to cities and towns, and hardwood timber for commercial uses. Pisgah is a vast land of high mountain peaks, dense forests and cascading waterfalls. Because its expanse spreads over different sections of WNC, it offers the visitor a great variety of terrain, plants and trees. Highways, forests roads and the Blue Ridge Parkway, make it accessible to everyone.

Pisgah National Forest acreage is found in the following counties: *Avery, Burke, Buncombe, Caldwell, Henderson, Haywood, Madison, McDowell, Mitchell, Transylvania, Watauga and Yancey.*

PISGAH NATIONAL FOREST POINTS OF INTEREST

Shining Rock   *Courtesy Forest Service*

SHINING ROCK WILDERNESS: Entrance permit required. A 13,600 acre tract in Haywood county named for the out-crops of huge glistening snow-white quartz on Shining Rock Mountain at 6,000 feet elevation. This is a primitive, remote retreat with outstanding scenery, fishing and hiking. There are 25 miles of hiking trails with 9 named and marked trails. Hiking distance and time can range from 0.3 miles and a 10 minute walk to the 6.7 miles of Greasy Cove Trail with over 4 hours walking time. All trails are signed at intersections and blazed with a footprint symbol except the Art Loeb Trail which is blazed with a yellow hiking symbol.

Permits and trail maps available at Pisgah District Ranger's Office on US 276 and from vendors on US 276 and NC 215. *Most visitors enter Shining Rock Wilderness from the Blue Ridge Parkway southwest of Asheville at Milepost 420. Take gravel road to parking area.*

LINVILLE GORGE WILDERNESS: Entrance permit required. Located in Burke and McDowell counties, this 7,600 acre tract is one of America's most scenic, rugged gorges, with swift waters, cliffs, deep pools, rapids and cascading waterfalls. Linville river descends more than 2,000 feet before entering the open flats of Catawba Valley. Ideal for primitive recreation, hiking, backpacking and rock climbing. Hunting and fishing permitted under state regulatons. Picnicking. Entrance permit and trail maps are available at District Ranger's Office, Marion, N.C. (Library Building.)

WISEMAN'S VIEW: Parking. Magnificent view of Linville Gorge. *Located off N.C. 105 near Linville Falls. Accessible from Blue Ridge Parkway and US 221. About 60 miles northeast of Asheville. Under 20 miles from Marion.*

ROAN MOUNTAIN RECREATION AREA. 600 acres of rhododendron gardens. Famed for outstanding display of purple rhododendron during June.

Roan Mountain (elevation 6,286) is a famous 7,000 acre recreation spot in Mitchell County. Picnicking, hiking, observation deck. *North of Bakersville off NC 261. Northeast of Asheville.*

LAKE POWHATAN. Located in Buncombe County south of Asheville. Surrounded by Bent Creek Experimental Forest where research is conducted for improving management of hardwood forests. National Forest Recreation area. Excellent family camping opportunity. 100 campsites. Picnicking, fishing, swimming beach with lifeguard, developed campground, nature trails. *Take N.C. 191 south from Asheville to Forest Service Road 3484 (under 10 miles from Asheville).*

CFA Campus Tour

In Pisgah Ranger District - U.S. 276 near Brevard

CRADLE OF FORESTRY IN AMERICA. First School of Forestry in America founded in 1898 in George Vanderbilt's Pisgah Forest in an area known as the Pink Beds. Visitor Center. One mile tour of "campus" demonstrations. *Located in Transylvania County between Brevard and Waynesville off US 276.*

THE FOREST FESTIVAL TRAIL: A new one mile trail developed in the Cradle of Forestry. This is a re-creation of "Biltmore Forest Fair," a 1908 excursion through the Biltmore Estate and Pisgah Forest. The trail demonstrates practical forestry with a display of seedling nurseries, lumbering techniques, a sawmill, logging train and trout pond. *Off US 276.*

SLIDING ROCK. 60 foot water covered rock slide used as a sliding board. Cold clear water below. *Off US 276. Late May through Labor Day.*

PISGAH ECOLOGY TRAIL. 45 minute educational tour located behind Pisgah Ranger Station. Self-guided tapes. *US 276.*

LOOKING GLASS FALLS. One of the most scenic, well-known falls in eastern U.S. Rush of water 30 feet wide dropping more than 60 feet down a sheer rock face into the pool below. *Adjacent to US 276.*

LOOKING GLASS ROCK. A granite monolith named because of glistening sides caused by water seeping from forest cover on top (elevation 3,967). Three mile foot trail from Davidson River Road.

NANTAHALA NATIONAL FOREST

Containing some 468,474 acres in seven counties of Southwestern North Carolina, the Nantahala National Forest is rich with lakes and waterfalls, rushing mountain streams and unlimited recreational opportunities. Bordering the Cherokee Indian Reservation, and originally the home of the Cherokee Indian nation, the Nantahala National Forest reflects Cherokee culture. There are geographical names such as the Tuckasegee and Oconaluftee Rivers. Nantahala is a Cherokee word meaning "Land of the Noonday Sun," a reference to the deep narrow valleys that receive the direct rays of the sun only at midday. During a time of friendship with early settlers, the famous Cherokee Chief Junaluska saved General Andrew Jackson's life in 1814 at the Battle of Horseshoe Bend in Alabama. The land of the Nantahala was Junaluska's home. He was born and buried in what is now Nantahala National Forest.

Nantahala National Forest acreage is found in the following counties: Cherokee, Clay, Graham, Jackson, Macon, Swain and Transylvania.

JOYCE KILMER-SLICKROCK WILDERNESS: No permit required. Characterized by large virgin timber, panoramic views and mountain streams, this 15,000 acre wilderness lies in the watersheds of Little Santeetlah Creek and Slickrock Creek in Graham County. Part of Joyce Kilmer Slickrock Wilderness is in the Cherokee National Forest in Tennessee. Mountain ridges rise over 5,000 feet in elevation. The Little Santeetlah Watershed includes the Joyce Kilmer Memorial Forest, established in 1936 as a memorial to Joyce Kilmer, author of the poem ***"Trees."*** Some of the huge trees are hundreds of years old; some are twenty feet around the base and more than a hundred feet high. The forest is abundant with wild life and plants, and has more than 60 miles of trails. Picnicking, hiking, fishing and hunting. *Accessible via US 129 north of Robbinsville, then NC 1116, NC 1127 and Forest Service Road 416. For more information contact District Ranger Station, Robbinsville.*

*Whiteside Mtn. from Whiteside Cove Road
Jackson County*

U.S. Forest Service Photo

WHITESIDE MOUNTAIN. *US 64 between Highlands and Cashiers.* Part of the Nantahala National Forest, Whiteside Mountain rises over 2,000 feet from the "valley floor". With its 800 foot sheer bluffs, Whiteside is reputed to be the highest sheer precipice in Eastern America. This long favored scenic attraction stands over the headwaters of the Chattooga River as it flows through Jackson County. The old toll road has been closed and a 2 mile loop trail constructed. A view from the summit at 4,930 feet affords views into 4 states - the Carolinas, Georgia, and Tennessee. Geologist believe Whiteside, composed of metamorphised granite, to be one of the oldest monoliths in the Americas. *From US 64 turn south on NC 1600 to the parking area. Hiking trail, overlook.*

Plan ahead to make your visit more fun and energy efficient; take advantage of the information brochures and trail maps available. If you are travelling a long distance for an outing, we recommend calling the Ranger Station in that area to verify directions. For detailed information write, call or visit:

U.S. Forest Service Visitor Information Office
50 South French Broad Avenue
P.O. Box 2750
Asheville, N.C. 28802
Phone: (704) 253-2352
(Open Mon.-Fri: 8:30-5:00)

You can also contact directly the Ranger District office for the area you plan to visit. The addresses and numbers are:

PISGAH NATIONAL FOREST

Pisgah Ranger District:
District Ranger
U.S. Forest Service
P.O. Box 8
  (US 276, 2 miles N. of Brevard)
Pisgah Forest, N.C. 28768
Phone: (704) 877-3265

Toecane Ranger District:
District Ranger
U.S. Forest Service
P.O. Box 128
  (US 19 By-pass in Burnsville)
Burnsville, N.C. 28714
Phone: (704) 682-6146

Grandfather Ranger District:
District Ranger
U.S. Forest Service
P.O. Box 519,
  (Library Building)
Marion, N.C. 28752
Phone: (704) 652-2144

French Broad Ranger District:
District Ranger
U.S. Forest Service
P.O. Box 128
  (US 25. ½ mile W. of
  Hot Springs)
Hot Springs, N.C. 28743
Phone: (704) 622-3202

NANTAHALA NATIONAL FOREST

Cheoah Ranger District:
District Ranger
U.S. Forest Service
Route 1, Box 16-A
  (US 129 N. of Robbinsville)
Robbinsville, N.C. 28771
Phone: (704) 479-6431

Tusquitee Ranger District:
District Ranger
U.S. Forest Service
201 Woodland Drive
  US 19 S. of Murphy)
Murphy, N.C. 28906
Phone: (704) 837-5152

Highlands Ranger District:
District Ranger
U.S. Forest Service
P.O. Box 749
  (US 64, Highlands)
Highland, N.C. 28741
Phone: (704) 526-3765

Wayah Ranger District:
District Ranger
U.S. Forest Service
Route 10, Box 210
  (US 64 W. of Franklin)
Franklin, N.C. 28734
Phone: (704) 524-6441

Scenic Asheville District   *Photo - National Park Service*

BLUE RIDGE PARKWAY

The Blue Ridge Parkway was created by an Act of Congress in 1936 as a recreational motor road connecting Shenandoah National Park in Virginia and Great Smoky Mountains National Park in North Carolina and Tennessee.

The Parkway was established to provide an elongated park for public use and enjoyment through safe, uninterrupted, leisure motor travel. A limited access roadway, speed is designed for 45 MPH and not for fast travel.

Public appreciation of this concept is reflected in annual visitation figures. Attracting as many as 16 million visitors in one year, the Parkway has become the most popular unit of the National Park System. The Parkway is administered by the National Park Service, a bureau of the U.S. Department of the Interior.

Winding for 470 miles along the crest of the Appalachians, the Parkway goes through the Blue Ridge, Black, Great Craggy, Great Balsam and Plott Balsam Mountain. Despite the hundreds of miles in length, the Parkway only encompasses some 78,174 acres. In North Carolina, over 44,000 acres extend through 17 counties.

Providing the visitor with some of the most diversified recreational experiences in America, the Parkway features and interprets the scenic, historical, natural and cultural resources of the region with emphasis on its rural character.

Great vistas in the highlands, small farms, mountain peaks, balsam forests and mountains of rhododendron are all part of a trip along the Parkway. Recreational features include camping, hiking, fishing, picnicking.

11

Parkway Activities   **Photo - National Park Service**

PARKWAY ACTIVITIES:

CAMPING. Ten recreational or developed areas for tents, trailers and RV's. Approximately 1100 campsites. Camping limited to 14 days. Supplies available at most Parkway service stations. No reservations for camping.

PICNIC GROUNDS. Easy trails, young and old can walk them without difficulty. Legstretchers taking 10 minutes to an hour. Trails described in official Parkway folder available on Parkway.

FISHING. Primarily Trout waters, Streams and Lakes along Parkway. State regulations apply. Temporary fishing licenses can be purchased by Parkway visitors. (Local hardware and sporting goods stores).

INTERPRETIVE ACTIVITIES: Summer programs in living history. Guided walks. Evening talks. Schedule listed on visitor activities sheet. Available on bulletin boards at Visitor Centers and developed sites.

Camping & Picnicking   **Photo - National Park Service**

VISITOR SEASON:

May *through* **October:** *Campgrounds, picnic areas and other accommodations open.*
June *through* **Labor Day:** *Full naturalist program in operation, guided and self-guided walks, evening nature talks, museum and roadside exhibits.*
Winter: *Can be delightful but roads may be closed because of hazardous driving conditions.*

THE FLOWERING SEASON:

Because of wide variations in elevation, peak blooming occurs at different times and places along the Parkway. The white dogwood begins to bloom in the bare forests in late April. The greening of spring shows on the mountains by mid-May when the Azalea, Rhododendron and Mountain Laurel begin their blooming period which can last until mid-June. Wildflowers are colorful throughout spring, summer and autumn. October is "leaf looking" time. Thousands of visitors drive up to see the mountains splashed with the rich golden colors of the Birch, Poplar, Buckeye and Beech trees and the red brilliance of **the Oak and Maples.**

The Arrowhead Symbol   **Photo - National Park Service**

The **Arrowhead** symbol identifies the National Park Service, an agency of the Department of the Interior. Symbol appears on entrance signs to Blue Ridge Parkway from major access highways.

 Emblem of Visitor Use Areas, with facilities such as camp-grounds, picnic areas, visitor centers exhibits, trails, food, gas, lodging and comfort station.

Interpretative signs carrying the squirrel gun and powder horn symbol will be found at various points along the Parkway where there is a legend, old building or place of scientific interest.
Mileposts mark the Parkway beginning with Milepost O near Waynesboro, Virginia, where the Parkway joins the Shenandoah National Park. Proceeding southwest and ending with Milepost 469, the Parkway enters the Great Smoky Mountains National Park near Cherokee, N.C.

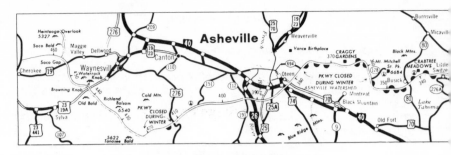

SPECIAL PLACES ON PARKWAY

VISITOR CENTERS. Focal points of the naturalist program. Each center features a different part of the region's natural or human history. Information available. Park Rangers on duty.

DOUGHTON PARK: *Milepost 238.5 to 274.7.* About 7,000 acres including campground, picnic areas, coffee shop, trails for hiking, auto service and Bluff's Lodge, one of four overnight facilities on Parkway. *Accessible by US 21 and NC 18 northeast of North Wilkesboro.*

BOONE BLOWING ROCK AREA: *Off US 321*
E. B. Jeffress Park: *Milepost 272.* Self-guiding trail to cascades. Picnic area.

MOSES H. CONE MEMORIAL PARK: *Milepost 292.7 to 295.* The Moses H. Cone House and 3,600 acre Estate maintained in its historical entirety. Two lakes, 25 miles of horse and carriage trails. Parkway Craft Center.

JULIAN PRICE MEMORIAL PARK: *Milepost 295 to 298.* 4,200 acres for recreation. Hiking trails. All year Campground - 100 sites. Picnic area. Lake and stream fishing.

LINVILLE FALLS: *Milepost 316.* Area purchased by John D. Rockefeller and donated to Parkway to insure protection and availability to visitors. Campgrounds. Trail to overlooks: Waterfalls, and Linville Gorge. Picnic area. *Located southwest of Linville and Grandfather Mountain. Ample parking.*

MOUNT MITCHELL STATE PARK: *Milepost 355.4. Highway NC 128 to Mt. Mitchell State Park.* Established in 1915, covering 1,469 acres, located on Mt. Mitchell (elev. 6,684), highest peak east of the Mississippi. Park extends along the ridges of the Black Mountains. Campgrounds, trails, picnic area, lookout tower. *In Yancey County, south of Burnsville.*

CRAGGY GARDENS: *Milepost 363.4 to 369.6.* Outstanding display purple Catawba Rhododendron. Peak of bloom in Mid-June. Trails, picnic area and Visitor Center. Short drive northeast of Asheville.

MOUNT PISGAH: *Milepost 408.6.* Part of George Vanderbilt's vast 100,000 acre estate. Campground, picnic area, trails, gas and supplies. Pisgah Inn and Restaurant.

RICHLAND BALSAM. *Milepost 431.* Self guiding trail. Highest point on the motor road. (Elev. 6,053 feet).

MUSEUM OF NORTH CAROLINA MINERALS: *Milepost 331.* Important stop. Building constructed with funds donated by the State of North Carolina, the Museum featues minerals and rare gem stones found in N.C.

Crabtree Falls - Mile Post 339

CRABTREE MEADOWS: *Milepost 339.* Beautiful Crabtree Falls. Picnic area. Campgrounds. Restaurant. Gas.

Brinegar Cabin   *National Park Service, Blue Ridge Parkway*

CRAFT SHOPS ON PARKWAY

BRINEGAR CABIN CRAFT SHOP. *Milepost 238.5. Located in Doughton Park.* Local handcrafts are sold in a charming cabin which is listed in the National Register of Historic Places. At Brinegar Cabin you will see a classic example of the self sufficiency of a typical 1890's mountain farm. Historic garden and outbuildings. *Midway between U.S. 21 and N.C. 18.*

NORTHWEST TRADING POST. *(elev. 3,000) Milepost 259. Glendale Springs, N.C. Open mid-April through October.* A gift shop sponsored by Northwest Development Association to preserve craft techniques and present fine products to the public. Over 258 different kinds of handmade crafts from 500 active artisans in 11 counties of Northwest North Carolina. Also antiques and homemade foods. All in a quaint cabin.

PARKWAY CRAFT CENTER. *Milepost 293.* A shop of the Southern Highland Handicraft Guild in the Moses Cone Manor House. Fine quality crafts. Boone-Blowing Rock area. *U.S. 321 access to Parkway. Craft demonstrations.*

FOLK ART CENTER. *Milepost 382 off US 70 at Oteen in Buncombe County near Asheville.* Offices and sales center for Southern Highland Handicraft Guild in impressive new building. Wide variety of exceptional crafts and furniture.

PISGAH INN. *Milepost 408.* Good selection of crafts and regional books. Shop located in Pisgah Inn and Restaurant complex, south of Asheville. *Parkway access US 25.*

Between Asheville & Pisgah   *Photo - Jack R. Gwennap*

LODGING ON PARKWAY

PISGAH INN: *Milepost 408. Blue Ridge Parkway. Phone (704) 235-8228.*
With an address like this at an elevation of 5,000 feet, the peak of the
Parkway is the place to be on a hot summer night. The Inn commands
a 360° sweep of ever changing scenery! From spring greening to October brilliance, the outlook from your private porch is dramatic. It will
be a memory to treasure. Comfort and hospitality are the by-words
here. Large rooms with two double beds. Reasonable family prices.
No charge for children under eight sharing the same room with
parents. Restaurant with panoramic view and good food. Look for
country ham and red eye gravy on the menu. In restaurant complex
you will also find a coffee shop and attractive craft shop. *Open May
through October. Located 25 miles south of Asheville. Also accessible
via US 276 from Brevard and Waynesville.*
For Reservations: Pisgah Inn *
   P.O. Box 749
Waynesville, N.C. 28787
Phone: (704) 235-8228.

PEAKS OF OTTER: *Milepost 85.6.* Lodge and restaurant (VA.)
ROCKY KNOB CABINS. *Milepost 174.* House Keeping cabins.
Rustic.(VA).
BLUFFS LODGE. *Milepost 241.* Lodge and Restaurant. (NC).

For additional Parkway information write to:
   Superintendent
   Blue Ridge Parkway
   700 Northwestern Bank Building
   Asheville, N.C. 28801

* adv.   17

WESTERN NORTH CAROLINA

COUNTIES

COUNTY	COUNTY SEAT	ALTITUDE (FEET)	COUNTY POPULATION
Alleghany	Sparta	2,939	9,570
Ashe	Jefferson	2,900	22,336
Avery	Newland	3,589	14,409
Buncombe	Asheville	2,216	160,934
Burke	Morganton	1,182	72,361
Caldwell	Lenior	1,182	67,391
Cherokee	Murphy	1,535	18,933
Clay	Hayesville	1,893	6,619
Graham	Robbinsville	2,150	7,217
Haywood	Waynesville	2,635	46,495
Henderson	Hendersonville	2,146	58,580
Jackson	Sylva	2,047	25,811
Macon	Franklin	2,113	20,178
Madison	Marshall	1,650	16,827
McDowell	Marion	1,437	35,135
Mitchell	Bakersville	2,550	14,428
Polk	Columbus	1,145	12,984
Rutherford	Rutherfordton	1,096	53,787
Swain	Bryson City	1,736	10,283
Transylvania	Brevard	2,230	23,417
Watauga	Boone	3,266	31,678
Wilkes	Wilkesboro	1,042	58,323
Yancey	Burnsville	2,817	14,934

AVERY COUNTY

Established 1911
County Seat: Newland. Elevation: 3,589 Ft.; Population: 14,409.
Places: **Linville, Grandfather Mountain.**
Created by an act of the State Legislature in 1911, Avery County is the youngest of the 100 counties of North Carolina. Containing 238 square miles, it includes the Toe River Valley and some of the highest mountains in Western North Carolina. With an average altitude of 3,000 feet, Avery is the highest county in the state. Young Avery County contains Grandfather Mountain (elv. 5,964) which geologists believe is the oldest mountain on earth. Spectacular scenery, natural beauty and the ski industry bring thousands of tourists to Avery County. Also mica mining, agriculture, dairy farming, manufacturing and the shrubbery business contribute to the economy.
EARLY HISTORY: Avery County was named for Colonel Waightstill Avery, Revolutionary hero and Attorney General 1777-79. The Newland area was an old Indian mustering ground long before the coming of the white man. The youngest county, the oldest mountain, and the highest average elevation in North Carolina, Avery is a county of superlatives.

LINVILLE AREA

ATTRACTIONS

GRANDFATHER MOUNTAIN ANNUAL EVENTS: Hang gliding competitions and demonstrations, Highland Games and Gathering of the Clans, Singing on the Mountain. Detailed material follows.
LINVILLE FALLS. *Blue Ridge Parkway Milepost 316.5.* Falls are situated in rugged mountain terrain. However, good hiking trails lead to overlooks of the falls and a gorge. Property was donated by John D. Rockefeller, Jr. Picnic area. *Just off Parkway and US 221 and NC 105.*
LINVILLE CAVERNS. *4 miles south of Parkway.* Many interesting formations in this brightly lighted cavern. Guided tours. *Open all year.*

View of Upper Falls   *Photo - National Park Service*

19

GRANDFATHER MOUNTAIN
U.S. 221 and Blue Ridge Parkway, Linville, N.C.

Grandfather Mountain is the highest peak in the Blue Ridge Mountains and features spectacular scenery of rugged rock formations dated by the U.S. Geological Survey as among the oldest on earth and of panoramic vistas of surrounding mountains and valleys stretching forth for over 100 miles.

The Mile-High Swinging Bridge on top of the mountain is Grandfather's most famous landmark and is only a few steps from the Visitor Center which includes exhibits of native wildflowers, minerals, mushrooms, and Indian artifacts, plus a mountain trout aquarium. Fifteen miles of hiking trails lead from the Visitor Center and the base of the mountain into the 4,100 acre recreational preserve.

Grandfather has two environmental habitats for Mildred The Bear and her family of Black Bears, a Cougar habitat, and a Deer habitat.

Hand gliding exhibition flights take place four times daily, May through October, weather permitting. A hang gliding movie filmed at Grandfather is shown during inclement weather.

The mountain is open daily April through mid-November and on good-weather weekends in the winter. The spring color season of May and June features wildflowers such as mountain laurel, flame azalea, vaseyi, and rhododendron, and from October 5-25, the mountain comes alive with a brilliant array of fall colors.

GRANDFATHER MOUNTAIN EARLY HISTORY. In 1794 Grandfather Mountain was visited by Andre Michaux, the renowned botanist. Reports of the lush growth and variety of wild flowers and plant life on the Appalachians had attracted the attention of the French Government. Michaux was sent to collect seeds for the royal garden at Versailles. A pioneer pursuit was developed by Michaux, who taught the mountain people how to gather and sell herbs. The medicinal herb Ginseng was prepared for the market in China and has remained a profitable item for the mountain people.

Grandfather Mountain was named by the Indians not for its old age but for the outline of rock formations and cliffs forming the image of a grandfather looking up into the sky. The grandfather can be seen as you approach the mountain on NC 105 about 10 miles south of Boone.

ANNUAL EVENTS AT GRANDFATHER MOUNTAIN

SINGING ON THE MOUNTAIN. *Fourth Sunday in June.* An old timey gospel sing, preaching, and family outing all rolled into one event. One of the largest annual events of its kind, the Singing celebrates its 58th anniversary in 1982. Tradition is strong at the Singing with popular TV and recording star Arthur Smith serving as music master for over 35 years. The main address is given by a nationally prominent speaker and some of the top gospel groups and individual entertainers in the country regularly appear. The event draws anywhere from 10,000 to 50,000 people depending on the weather and personalities appearing.

Hang-gliding off Grandfather Mountain   *Photo - Hugh Morton*

MASTERS OF HANG GLIDING CHAMPIONSHIP. *Mid-September, a six-day event.* The top 28 pilots in the world compete by invitation based on competative records in one of the premiere tournaments in this new and beautiful sport. The mountain's lofty peaks and magnificent scenery make for an ideal setting to determine the best hang glider pilot in the world. Spectators can watch launches at the top and landings at MacRae Meadow.

Highland Games

HIGHLAND GAMES & GATHERING OF SCOTTISH CLANS. *Second weekend in July.* The outstanding event of its kind in the United States. Scotsmen (and Scotsmen at heart) come from all over the world to participate in the athletic competition, dances, and piping, or just to watch the festivities and visit the colorful clan tents that surround MacRae Meadow where the Games are held. Related concerts and social activities abound during the evenings. All this against the backdrop of Grandfather Mountain is dramatic, bold, and beautiful. Write: *Grandfather Mountain Highland Games, Linville, N.C. 28646 after March 1,* to receive a colorful flyer on the Games.

LODGING AND SHOPS

SMOKETREE INN AND LODGE. *Hwy. 105 between Linville and Boone. (704)963-4776.*
SUGAR MT. LODGE. *Hwy. 184 between Linville and Boone. (704)898-4521.*
TOP OF BEECH MT. INN. *Banner Elk, N.C. (704)387-2252.*
VILLAGE INN AT BEECH MT. *Banner Elk, N.C. (704)387-4221.*
ESEEOLA LODGE. *Linville, N.C. (704)733-4311.*

CREATIVE CRAFTS. *Hwy.105 between Linville and Boone.* Across from Seven Devils. Referred to as the "Valley Shop," this rustic log cabin craft shop has Grandfather Mountain as a backdrop. Quality mountain crafts - handmade toys, fine quilts, canopies, dulcimers, pottery, items of wood. Relaxed atmosphere. *Open all year. Daily 9 to 5:30. Sunday afternoons.* Another Creative Crafts shop on *Blowing Rock Rd., Hwy. 321.*

COUNTRY HOUSE VILLAGE. *Hwy. 105 at Fasco.* Small complex. Outstanding here is the **Iron Mountain Stoneware Factory Store.** Pottery from one of the nation's best stoneware manufacturers. Many patterns in dinnerware, planters, mugs and table accessories.

GREEN MANSIONS VILLAGE. *Hwy. 105.* Complex that includes **Country Gourmet, Nordic House, Mountain Peddler.**

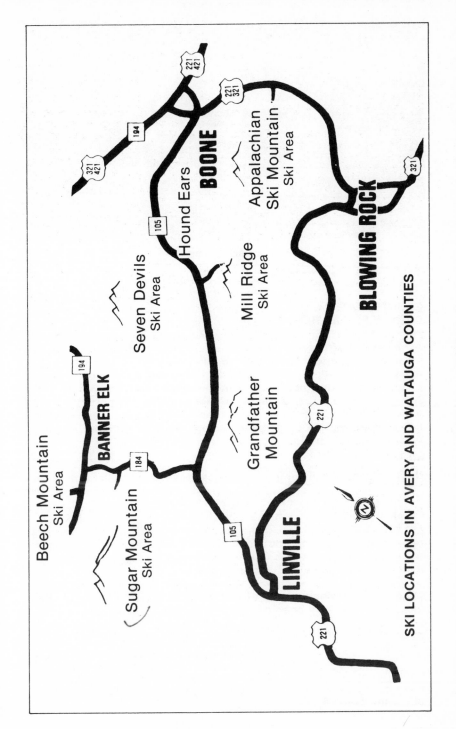

SKI LOCATIONS IN AVERY AND WATAUGA COUNTIES

Beech Mountain
Ski Area

Sugar Mountain
Ski Area

BANNER ELK

Seven Devils
Ski Area

Hound Ears

BOONE

Appalachian
Ski Mountain
Ski Area

Mill Ridge
Ski Area

BLOWING ROCK

Grandfather
Mountain

LINVILLE

23

Downtown Asheville, N. C.   **"The Land of the Sky"**   *Photo by Phyllis Vance*

BUNCOMBE COUNTY
Established 1792

COUNTY SEAT: *Asheville, Elevation 2,216 Ft.*
COUNTY POPULATION: *160,934*
PRINCIPAL TOWNS: *Asheville, Black Mountain, Weaverville.*

Asheville is the largest city in Western North Carolina. Fine interstate highways lead into the city. I-40 from the east and west, and I-26 from the southeast. The Blue Ridge Parkway weaves in and out over the mountain tops but dips down conveniently at 6 access points in the Asheville area. The Asheville-Hendersonville Airport (south of Asheville via US 25 and I-26) serves the Asheville area. Long a recreation and convention center, Asheville is the mountain metropolis of Western North Carolina.

HISTORY:

Until 1783 the vast mountain wildernes of Western North Carolina was part of the Cherokee Nation and forbidden to white settlers. A 1767 treaty, signed by the Cherokees and the British Governor of North Carolina, William Tryon, had established the crest of the Blue Ridge as the boundary line between the races. As a result, colonial development of the North Carolina mountains was halted by a distant Governor living in eastern North Carolina and separated geographically and politically from the land hungry pioneers.

In spite of formidable natural barriers and British intervention, the mountains had long been penetrated by white men. Explorers came with Hernando De Soto in 1540, and botanists, hunters and trappers came in later years. Trade with the Indians motivated the earliest known travelers into Western North Carolina. Deerskins were in great demand for eighteenth century European fashion. Traders from South Carolina and Virginia set up factors or trading posts in Indian villages. Also, hardy pioneers had pushed westward and built isolated farms along the great rivers.

During the Revolutionary War, the Cherokees continued to be allied with the British. Defending their homeland and hunting grounds, the Cherokee warriors went on the warpath in June 1776 planning complete extermination of the white man. This action was met with retaliation by the forces of Virginia and the Carolinas and in September 1776, General Griffith Rutherford commanded a North Carolina force of 2400 men. Crossing the Blue Ridge in Cherokee country by way of the Swannanoa Gap and the French Broad River (in present Asheville), General Rutherford moved westward to destroy over sixty villages and towns of the Cherokee, thus sealing the fate of the proud Cherokee Nation.

Following the Revolutionary War, Tryon's treaty was null and void. In 1783 the new state of North Carolina opened the mountain region and issued land grants to settlers. In 1784 the first effort at permanent settlement in Buncombe County was made by Samuel Davidson, a young veteran who crossed the Blue Ridge from Fort Davidson (present Old Fort) through the Swannanoa Gap. With his wife, child and servant, he cleared land and built a cabin near the Swannanoa River. Before spring planting, he was killed by a hunting party of Cherokees, and his small family retreated down the mountain to the safety of the fort. Samuel Davidson's brother William and other family members returned to avenge his death. They remained and formed the Swannanoa settlement.

Other scattered settlements developed nearby, and in 1792, the new county of Buncombe, named for Revolutionary General Edward Buncombe, was established from western portions of Burke and Rutherford. So extensive was this new county that it was called the "State of Buncombe." In 1797 the town of Asheville was incorporated, and the "Buncombe Turnpike" was opened in 1827. A fine dirt highway following the French Broad River, it was considered "the best in the State," and replaced old muddy trails connecting Tennessee and South Carolina.

In the middle 1800's, Asheville was a noisy young farming community thriving from busy commerce. Much business was generated by the movement of thousands of domestic animals driven in autumn through Asheville to southern markets. The eventful Civil War years saw families alienated over divided loyalties, and the Buncombe Riflemen formed the first company of men to leave Asheville for service in Virginia.

With the arrival of the railroad in 1880, visitors brought prosperity, and the mountains were infused with a cosmopolitan influence that still remains to enrich the quality of life in Western North Carolina.

For more information:
Asheville Area Chamber of Commerce
151 Haywood St.,
Asheville, NC 28802
(704) 258-5200

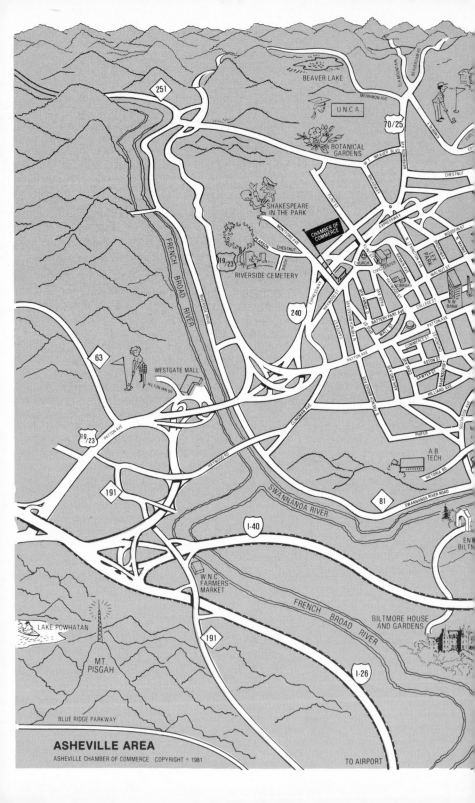

ASHEVILLE AREA

ASHEVILLE CHAMBER OF COMMERCE COPYRIGHT © 1981

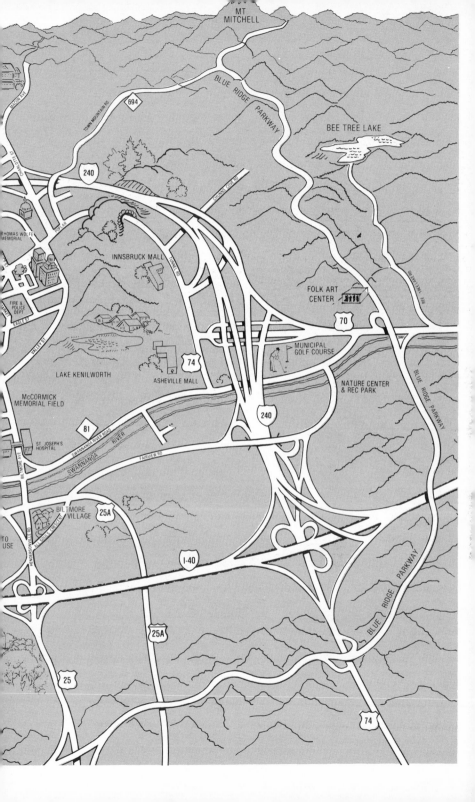

AKZONA BUILDING
I.M. PEI - Architect
Dedicated July, 1981

ASHEVILLE, NORTH CAROLINA
ANNUAL EVENTS IN THE CIVIC CENTER

Mid-March: Mountain Youth Festival - Traditional Mountain Music and Dancing.
Late March or Early April: Annual Art Museum Auction.
Early April: Blue Ridge Gun Show.
Mid-June: Chapman's Antiques Fair.
Mid-July: Southern Highlands Handicraft Guild Fair.
Early August: Asheville Antiques Fair.
Early August: Mountain Dance and Folk Festival.
Mid-August: High Country Craft Summerfest Show.
Mid-August: Blue Ridge Gun Show.
Mid-October: Southern Highlands Handicraft Guild Fair.
Late November: High Country Crafters Mountain Christmas Show.

Haywood Street Box Office Phone; 255-5771.

CRAFTSMAN'S FAIR — *July, Civic Center, Haywood St.*

In 1930 the Southern Highland Handicraft Guild was formed to answer the needs of the mountain people. A forum to present their skills to wide exposure became a reality. For many years the craftsmen had produced all the necessary products for rural households. Not only furniture and clothing but also cookware, baskets, tools and toys were made at home. With the development of manufactured goods, however, many skills were in danger of being lost.

By the late 1920's concerned individuals determined to preserve and continue craft knowledge. Modern marketing techniques as well as general management helped to make the movement successful.

The Southern Highland Handicraft Guild sponsors the Craftsman's Fair for a week in July in Asheville.

Mountain Dance and Folk Festival   Photo - Phyllis Vance

MOUNTAIN DANCE AND FOLK FESTIVAL. *Civic Center-August.* Sponsored by the Folk Heritage Committee of the Asheville Area Chamber of Commerce, this Festival began in 1927 and has continued to receive enthusiastic support and participation. Dancers and musical performers come from miles around to enjoy and produce what has become one of the outstanding folk festivals of the nation. Lonesome ballads and lively tunes have been kept alive from other centuries. Join the crowd "Along about Sundown"; you'll have an exciting evening as you watch and listen to the very best in fiddling, picking and dancing. *First Thursday-Friday-Saturday in August.*

RECREATION

Shindig City/County Plaza   **Photo - Phyllis Vance**

SHINDIG-ON-THE-GREEN

Sponsored and produced by the Folk Heritage Committee of the Asheville Area Chamber of Commerce, this summer time performance of square-dancing happens on the City/County Plaza in downtown Asheville. Several teams of square dancers perform each Saturday night, and informal street dancing offers the audience a chance to participate. Casual, relaxed and happy describes the atmosphere. Great-circle square, clog and buck dancing are executed. Musical instruments are fiddle, dulcimer, banjo and dobro. Sometimes folk stories for children. *Shindig begins on the first Saturday in July at 7:30 p.m. and continues through August. No admission.*

LAKE JULIAN PARK. *N.C. 280 off US 25.* Open all year from 8 am till the sun goes down. Fishing boats for rent by hour or day. Sailboat club or sailboating per day (bring your own). Fishing license required. Fenced-in playground, picnic tables, wild ducks to enjoy and feed. Operated by the Buncombe County Parks and Recreation (non-profit). *Off US 25 south of Asheville, turn at Skyland to NC 280, entrance opposite Valley Springs School. Developed Campground.* Phone: (704) 684-0376.

Recreation con't Asheville

GREATER ASHEVILLE AREA GOLF COURSES
Asheville Municipal Golf. Asheville, N. C. Ph: 704/298-1867
Great Smokies Hilton. Asheville, N. C. Ph: 704/254-3211
Mount Mitchell Golf Club. Burnsville, N. C. Ph: 704/675-5454
Springdale Country Club. Canton, N. C. Ph: 704/235-8451
Maggie Valley Country Club. Maggie Valley, N. C. Ph: 704/926-1616.
Waynesville Country Club. Waynesville, N. C. Ph: 704/456-3551
Wolf Laurel Golf Course. Mars Hill, N. C. Ph: 704/689-4111.
Fairfield Sapphire Valley Club. Sapphire, N. C. Ph: 704/743-3441.
Sherwood Forest Golf Course. Cedar Mountain, N. C. Ph: 704/885-2091.
HENDERSONVILLE COURSES
Crooked Creek Golf Course. Kanuga Rd.
Etowah Valley Golf Course. US 64.
Lost Diamond Valley Club. Hwy. US 25 and NC 176.

TENNIS

ASHEVILLE RACQUET CLUB. *200 Racquet Club Rd. US 25 S. 274-3361.*
Seven days until 10 p.m. Buster Brown, nationally ranked tennis professional, and the Asheville Racquet Club are a winning combination. The ARC has a great setup for tennis enthusiasts. All year, all weather indoor and outdoor courts. Family and individual memberships available, or rates by the hour. Handball, racquetball and a pool are part of the enjoyment. Also health club, saunas and Bell's Tennis Shop.
TENNIS—HILTON RESORT. Four indoor brushed laykold courts and four outdoor fast-dri Rubico courts. Tennis pro - ball machines - video instruction and saunas.
ASTON PARK TENNIS CENTER. *Hilliard Ave. at South French Broad. 255-5193 or 255-5436.* Twelve lighted composition courts open to public March - November. Nominal fee charged after 4 p.m. weekdays and all day weekends and holidays. Annual City of Asheville Tennis Tournament conducted third week of July.
T.C. ROBERSON HIGH SCHOOL. *Overlook Road, Skyland (South Asheville) 684-8040.* Open to public after school hours. First come — first serve — no pun intended. In fact, the six consolidated High Schools in Buncombe County have tennis courts open to the public.

SKI AREAS

APPALACHIAN SKI MOUNTAIN. *Blowing Rock, N.C. US 321. Ph: (704)295-7828. French-Swiss Ski College. Write: P.O. Box 106, Blowing Rock, N.C. 28605.*
HOUND EARS: *Blowing Rock, N.C. Hwy. 105. Ph: (704)963-4321.*
BEECH MOUNTAIN: *Rt. 1330 North Banner Elk, N.C. Ph: (704)387-2011.*
SUGAR MOUNTAIN: *Hwy. 184, Banner Elk, N.C. Ph: (704)963-5365.*
SEVEN DEVILS: *Hwy. 105. Banner Elk, N.C. Ph: (704)963-4305.*
MILL RIDGE: *Hwy. 105, Banner Elk, N.C. Ph: (704)693-4500.*
CATALOOCHEE: *Maggie Valley, N.C. Ph:(704)926-0285.*
SAPPHIRE VALLEY: *Hwy. 64. Sapphire, N.C. Ph: (704)743-3441.*
SCALY. *Hwy. 106, Highlands, N.C. Ph: (704)526-3737.*
WOLF LAUREL: *Off Hwy. 23., Mars Hill, N.C. Ph: (704)689-4111.*

31

MUSEUMS — HISTORIC BUILDINGS

Photo - A. Hawthorne

FOLK ART CENTER *of the Southern Highland Handicraft Guild. On the Blue Ridge Parkway east of Asheville, NC. Milepost 382.* More than 600 members of the Guild live in the nine state Southern Highland region, and their products are sold in the Folk Art Center. Special exhibitions are planned and shown on a regular basis. An active educational program offers classes, seminars and workshops. In a beautiful setting, the Folk Art Center is visually attractive both inside and outside. Open to the public every day except Christmas and New Year's Day 9 to 5. Folk Art Center memberships are available to everyone and members will receive mailings for schedules and events. Mailing address: *Box 9545, Asheville, N.C. 28815.*

ASHEVILLE ART MUSEUM — *Civic Center Lower Level. Closed Mondays. Tel. 253-3227.* Continuous variety of outstanding exhibits — well recognized touring shows and loans from prestigious museums. A growing permanent collection and fine art on loan. A beautiful and newly installed special gallery housing an extraordinary collection of weapons and armor. *Tues.-Sat. and Sunday afternoon.*

COLBURN MINERAL MUSEUM — *Civic Center Lower Level. Closed Mondays.* An extensive collection of minerals, fossils of the area. Native gem stones and a collection of fabulous replicas of the famous diamonds of the world. Well lighted and displayed. Informed staff to help guide you. *Tues.-Sat. and Sunday afternoon.*

THE HEALTH ADVENTURE. An exciting trip into the world of good health. Tours available for visitors of all ages. A small admission fee is requested and reservations are required. *Located at MAHEC Building, 501 Biltmore Ave. Call 254-6373 for information and reservations. Gift Shop.*

Thomas Wolfe Memorial   Photo - Nick Lanier

⎩THE THOMAS WOLFE MEMORIAL
Registered National Historic Landmark, North Carolina State Historic Site, entered National Register of Historic Places

THE THOMAS WOLFE MEMORIAL 48 *Spruce Street. Open all year. 253-8304. Open Tuesday - Saturday. 9 am to 5 pm and Sunday afternoon.* Operated by the North Carolina Division of Archives and History, Thomas Wolfe's boyhood home is one of two State Historic Sites in the Asheville area (the other is the Vance Birthplace near Weaverville, N.C.). Built in 1883 and expanded through the years to become a 28-room house, the Thomas Wolfe Memorial reflects the furnishings and boarding house lifestyle of the early 1900's. Purchased in 1906 by the author's mother, Julia Wolfe, the building is one of the oldest houses in downtown Asheville. It retains charming Queen Anne details including a slate shingled roof and colored glass inserts in the windows. Much of the same furniture, cooking utensils and china used by Mrs. Wolfe ("Mrs. Eliza Gant") is on display. Thomas Wolfe, Asheville's most famous literary figure, immortalized the boarding house, "Old Kentucky Home" where he lived for ten years before leaving in 1916 for college in Chapel Hill and graduate school at Harvard. Thomas Wolfe's sensitive first novel *Look Homeward Angel* was published in 1929, shocking the town with its thinly disguised characters who people the fictitious boarding house "Dixieland" and "Altamont," his beloved Asheville. Well informed guides will show you the Thomas Wolfe Memorial. Thomas Wolfe books sold. Nominal fee. Group rates.

33

Vance Birthplace   *Photo - Nick Lanier*

VANCE BIRTHPLACE STATE HISTORIC SITE. *Reems Creek Rd., Weaverville, N.C. (704) 645-6706. U.S. 19-23 North of Asheville. Follow signs.* Born May 13, 1830, Zebulon Baird Vance was one of the great men of North Carolina. At the age of twenty-four Vance served in the North Carolina House of Commons. At twenty-seven he was elected to the first of two terms in the United States Congress. First a Captain of the "Rough and Ready Guards" and later a Colonel during the Civil War, Vance was elected to the first of three terms as governor. After the war he served three full terms as United States Senator and died during his fourth term. The historic restoration of the birth place includes the original chimney and two original fireplaces, some paneling, flooring, rafters and foundation rock. Three times the size of the average mountain log house, it was considered a showplace. *12 miles northeast of Asheville. Open Tuesday-Saturday 9 A.M. - 5 P.M. Sunday 1 P.M. - 5 P.M. Closed Monday. Pioneer Days, third Sundays in April and September.*

Smith - McDowell House   *Photo - Nick Lanier*

SMITH McDOWELL HOUSE (c. 1840)
National Register of Historic Places

WESTERN NORTH CAROLINA HERITAGE CENTER *283 Victoria Road, Asheville, N.C. 28801, 253-9231. Open June through October. Tuesday through Saturday 10 am to 4 pm. Sunday 1 to 5 pm. Open November through May for scheduled events.* Entered on the National Register of Historic Places in 1975, the Smith-McDowell House has been restored by the Western North Carolina Historical Association as a Museum and Heritage Center. The three story Smith-McDowell House was constructed by local craftsmen in 1840. One of the oldest and finest brick buildings in Asheville, it was located near the Buncombe Turnpike, the principal thoroughfare connecting Tennessee and South Carolina in the mid 1800's. Prominent features of the house include the double front porch supported by slender columns, four massive chimneys, a kitchen wing and carriage entrance. James McConnell Smith, builder of the house, was the first white child born in what is now the City of Asheville. His father, Colonel Daniel Smith, was one of the region's first settlers. In 1974 this historic property was acquired by the Asheville Buncombe Technical College. To insure its preservation the house was leased to the Western North Carolina Historical Association for restoration and establishment of a regional historical and cultural center. The purpose of the center is "to preserve and perpetuate the history and cultural heritage of the mountain region of North Carolina...to keep alive the past...to enrich the future." Group tours by reservation. Admission charged. Follow A-B Tech signs to 283 Victoria Road.

HISTORIC BUILDINGS

St. Lawrence Catholic Church

ST. LAWRENCE CATHOLIC CHURCH *entered in National Register of Historic Places. 97 Haywood Street - opposite Civic Center. Tel. 252-6042. Call for Visitor Information.* An architectural wonder, St. Lawrence Church was begun in 1900 and completed in 1909. It has an elliptical dome which is entirely self-supporting and is built of tiles. The church was designed by Raphael Guastavino, a noted Spanish architect; its prototype was a church of the Baroque period in Valencia, Spain.

FIRST BAPTIST CHURCH. *Oak and Woodfin Streets. Entered on the National Register of Historic Places 1976.* The history of the First Baptist Church in Asheville began in 1829 when the first log building was erected on borrowed ground. The present church sanctuary, built in 1926, was designed by the noted architect Douglas Ellington and remains as one of several Asheville buildings which are outstanding in their architectural interpretation of the style of the mid 1920's. *Phone 252-4781 for services and activities.*

CHURCH STREET, so named since 1870, where some of Asheville's earliest congregations established their church homes.

CENTRAL UNITED METHODIST CHURCH (c. 1837). *27 Church Street. 253-3316.*

FIRST PRESBYTERIAN CHURCH (c. 1841). *40 Church Street. 253-1431.*

TRINITY EPISCOPAL CHURCH. (c. 1849). *Church Street. 253-9361.*

MUSEUMS (con't)

Nature Center

WESTERN NORTH CAROLINA NATURE CENTER. *Located at the Recreation Park. Gashes Creek Road, off NC 81 in Southeast Asheville, 298-5600. Tues.-Sat. and Sunday afternoon.* An educational facility designed to stimulate awareness and knowledge of the fascinating world of nature. "World of Night" (Nocturnal Hall), "World of Sea" (Marine display), a nature museum and live exhibits. Nature Park has animal burrows in "World Underground," and nature trails. Educational Mini-Farm with a diversity of farm animals and plants and exhibitions. Telephone the above number for educational programs for prescheduled groups. Small fee charged. Nature program every Sunday at 3:00 pm.

THE UNIVERSITY OF NORTH CAROLINA AT ASHEVILLE
University Heights off U.S. 25 N. Ph: 258-6600

UNCA is an outgrowth of Buncombe County Junior College which was founded in 1927 as North Carolina's first junior college. Now with an enrollment of over 2,000 students and 18 departments, U.N.C.A. offers a 4 year education in the liberal arts and sciences as well as some professional programs. Facilities include the 198 acre campus and 21 buildings including men's and women's dormitories.

(UNIVERSITY BOTANICAL GARDENS)

These gardens represent a force for the preservation of the native flora of North Carolina. Ten acres of gardens on the campus of the University of North Carolina-Asheville contain 26,000 native plants. Streams and bridges accent the beauty and variety of labeled plants, trees and flowers of the southern Appalachians. One focal point on tour is a "dog-run" cabin typical of the two room structures constructed by the earliest settlers. Sculpture garden for the blind. Trail through woods leads past earth works and marker of the Civil War Battle of Asheville. *For guided tours call: 667-1252. No admission charge. Follow the sign off Merrimon Ave. US 25 N.*

CRAFTS

ALLANSTAND. *16 College St. Tel. 253-2051. Mon.-Sat.* Asheville is indeed fortunate to have Southern Highland Handicraft Guild Shops. Allanstand is one of the oldest and finest. A fine collection of sculptures, ceramics, metal works and woodcarvings among many other beautiful things. Don't miss it.

GUILD CRAFTS. *930 Tunnel Road, US 70. 298-7903. Mon.-Sat.* The Southern Highland Handicraft Guild is famous for marketing quality crafts of the Southern Appalachians. This is one of the official craft shops of the Guild, so look for beauty and excellence in craftsmanship. Woodcarving, jewelry, pottery, and handwoven woolens. *Located 3 miles east of the Asheville Tunnel.*

HIGH COUNTRY CRAFTERS. *29 Haywood St. Tel. 254-0700. Mon.-Sat.* More than 170 Mountain craftsmen and artists have banded together to bring you unique handcrafted works. Sculptures, weaving, quilts, dulcimers, nature craft, wooden toys, hand built and wheel thrown pottery, marquetry, candles and leather.

THE SPINNING WHEEL. *1096 Hendersonville Rd. Rt. 25 S. 274-0720.* Started in 1924 by the late Miss Clem Douglas, a leading guardian of the craft heritage, this shop continues its tradition of excellence. Outstanding are the woven and woolen items and pottery (stoneware). There is a beautiful supply of marquetry — pictures made from wood inlay. Attractive log cabin with well displayed crafts.

COUNTRY BOUTIQUE. *Mars Hill College Campus. 689-2050.* An ancient log cabin houses this marvelous collection of handmade mountain crafts. Dolls, carvings, furniture, baskets, quilts and toys.

STUART NYE JEWELRY. *940 Tunnel Road, US 70. 298-7988. Mon.-Fri.* This is a workshop making beautiful hand-wrought silver and copper jewelry. In 1933 with a few second hand tools, some silver and good taste, Stuart Nye started producing delicate flowers and leaves in silver. The dogwood is the most famous of hundreds of designs.

BROWN'S POTTERY. *US 25 S. Arden.* Native clay in French style flameproof cookware.

EVAN'S POTTERY. *Clayton Rd., Arden.* Handthrown clay items by sixth generation potters.

PISGAH FOREST POTTERS. *Brevard Rd., NC 191.*

BILTMORE INDUSTRIES. The Biltmore Industries began as a club for young people in All Soul's Church in Biltmore Village. Classes were started in woodcarving, needlework and weaving. Old looms were rediscovered and many persons were put to work. Some carded; others did the dyeing, spinning and weaving in isolated places on the Biltmore Estate. In 1905 Mrs. George Vanderbilt organized this project into a regular industry which encouraged the mountain people's natural aptitude in crafts. The industry was sold to Fred Seely in 1917 and was moved from Biltmore Village to its present location in the charming old English type buildings on the Grove Park Inn grounds. Take time to see homespun created from raw fleece-to-loom-to-finished fabric. **LOCATED ON GROVE PARK INN GROUNDS.**

ESTES WINN ANTIQUE CAR MUSEUM. Next door to Biltmore Industries.

HOTELS & RESORTS

Photo Courtesy Asheville Chamber of Commerce

GROVE PARK INN AND COUNTRY CLUB
Entered on National Register of Historic Places

HISTORY: *The hotel was built by E. W. Grove, a research chemist who patented the medicine Bromo-Quinine. On a visit to Asheville in 1906, Mr. Grove initiated a residential development called Grove Park. He also conceived the idea of building a fine hotel on Sunset Mountain. Built in eleven months without an architect or contractor, the finished hotel fulfilled Mr. Grove's vision. The massive structure was built with huge boulders dredged from Sunset Mountain. The great lobby is one hundred feet long and twenty four feet high. Grove Park represents a remarkable feat of engineering.*

GROVE PARK INN AND COUNTRY CLUB. North Asheville on Sunset Mountain. From East-West I-240 take Charlotte Street exit. Inn open April to November, Country Club open year round. One of the South's outstanding resort hotels since 1913. 18-hole golf course available to hotel guests. In season, dining on the fabulous open-air Sunset Terrace, overlooking Asheville and the Blue Ridge Mountains. Nightly entertainment. Specialties include mountain trout, prime rib, home-baked breads, French pastries. Terrace open to public for lunch and dinner, reservations suggested. *290 Macon Ave., Asheville, NC, 28804. Tel. (704) 252-2711.* *

* adv.

Inn on Plaza   **Photo - RTM**

SMOKY MOUNTAINS INN ON THE PLAZA. *One Thomas Wolfe Plaza, Asheville, N.C. 28807. Ph.: (704) 252-8211. Toll free (800) 438-3960 outside N.C. Toll free (800) 222-0859 inside N.C.* A deluxe full-service hotel located in the heart of downtown Asheville and nestled between the mountains of Western North Carolina - a prime location that is convenient to local highways. The Inn on the Plaza is Asheville's newest and largest hotel, with facilities for conventions, meetings, special banquets and other large gatherings. The Inn on the Plaza offers a special plan and services for the corporate traveler, while still making sure that vacationers are equally well cared for and feel welcome. The hotel has three excellent restaurants, a night club, and a lobby bar - all provide a variety of foods and atmospheres. Nightly entertainment in the Pipkin, the hotel's lobby bar, and in Grosvenors, the elegant roof-top restaurant. Breakfast and lunch are served daily in Delmonico's. New Orlean's style seafood is available in the Half-Shell, the hotel's informal seafood and oyster bar. Guest services include a swimming pool, laundry service, airline ticket reservations, gift-shop, newsstand, messenger service, and on-site parking. The Thomas Wolfe Memorial is located next door to the hotel, and tours of the Biltmore House and Gardens are available. Owned and operated by Beaumont Hotels. *

40   * adv.

Great Smokies Hilton Resort   *Photo - Great Smokies Hilton*

GREAT SMOKIES HILTON RESORT. *One Hilton Inn Drive, Asheville, NC 28806. Phone (704) 254-3211.* This resort complex offers much to its guests. The location, barely a mile from downtown Asheville, is convenient and easy to reach whether you are driving via one of the two interstate highways or arriving from the airport. The resort has 200 acres beautifully landscaped. Of Spanish influenced contemporary design, the hotel is handsome and presents a visual welcome on approach. The central building and three guest wings are constructed of native stone and conform to the contour of the rolling terrain. Really spacious rooms look out on the golf course and mountains. Side-by-side suites and bilevel suites with fireplaces are available. There is a Hilton Family Plan, so if you are traveling with children (regardless of age), there is no extra charge when the same room is occupied. Small or large meetings, receptions, weddings and banquets can be easily arranged. There are nine conference centers and a ballroom accommodating up to 950. An inviting porch-type restaurant enclosed in glass offers green vistas. As a remembrance of other days, it is called "Aunt Minnie's Wisdom." If you're feeling frisky or just want to watch and enjoy, drop into the Library Lounge after dinner. A sprawling 18 hole golf course, 8 tennis courts (four enclosed) and two swimming pools round out this complete resort facility. A newsstand-gift shop ∗

* adv.   41

AS YOU SEE, NO MATTER WHICH WAY YOU ARE GO-
ING *Round the Mountain* YOU CAN GET TO:

WESTGATE SHOPPING CENTER

*Easy come and easy go, on a cloverleaf to
Westgate & the Great Smokies Hilton Hotel
and Country Club.* You will be saying,"What
a place for a shopping center. Convenient
and comfortable. 26 places of business all
within a few steps of each other."

RAZZBERRY'S *ice cream*	WARREN HEATON,LTD.
DOWNEY'S DINER	*jr. apparel*
THE SHRIMP BOAT	TURNTABLE
MEYERS/ARNOLD	SHERMAN'S SPORTS
department store	WESTGATE TOY & HOBBY
LONDONTOWN	WESTERN AUTO SUPPLY
london fog outlet	FAN'S GALORE!
HALF PRICE HOUSE	RADIO SHACK
women's apparel	REVCO
FABRIC BOUTIQUE	THE TAILOR SHOP
custom sewing	*alterations*
KINNEY'S SHOES	WESTGATE BARBER SHOP
LIB'S CARDS	GUYS & GALS
GORDON'S JEWELERS	*hair styling*
PARK'S FLOWERS	FUNLAND
P. ROSE *variety*	*electronic games*
	NCNB *branch bank*

WELCOME TO WESTGATE

SHOPPING FOR ANTIQUES, HOUSE AND GARDEN*

COLLECTOR'S CORNER. *68 North Market St. 252-2015.* Owners Polly and Paul Hicklin have a prime location just a short walk from Inn on the Plaza and Sheraton Hotels. Usual and unusual in antiques. A nice collection with variety - period and primitive furniture, paintings, rugs, china, silver etc.

THE UNICORN GALLERIES. *70 North Market St. Mon.-Sat. 10:30-5:30. Ph: 253-8118.* An antique shop offering beautiful furniture and decorator accessories in a bright attractive showroom. Unusual lamps and shades - custom design and repair of lamps. Choice selections for your home or for that special wedding gift.

CORNER CUPBOARD ANTIQUES. *959 Merrimon Ave. Ph: 258-9815.* Victorian furniture is popular again and this is the place to find it. Unusual collection of art glass and R.S. Prussia. Variety of hard to find pieces at moderate prices. Special group of investment quality pieces.

THE COUNTRY TOUCH *at the Biltmore Country Market, 1000 Hendersonville Rd., U.S. 25 South (704) 274-5410.* Mon.-Sat., An authentic hand hewn log cabin is the charming background for country antiques, handmade gifts, pine cone wreaths and ornaments. Also decorative accessories and accent pieces of old copper, tools, pewter and glass.

FIREPLACE ANTIQUES. *See Biltmore Village.*

AMBIANCE INTERIORS. *27 Broadway. 253-9403.* Kathryn S. Long, ASID, professional member, has established a design firm offering both residential and commercial services. In addition to representing a vast range of fiber, wallcovering, and furniture resources, the firm also does space planning. Ambiance specializes in architectural remodeling and addition, adaptive re-use, kitchen planning. The beautiful showroom is a delight to browsers, and you will be inspired to give your environment a new look. Accessories include baskets from all over the world.

THELMA LOU'S. *29 Broadway. 258-2328.* The freshest ideas in contemporary furnishings are here. Flexible lighting to enliven every interior area, frames, posters for your walls, and chairs and tables that can be mixed and matched to make your own Look. Chairs that go inside or out, simple upholstered sofas and chairs, storage units for walls, sisal and rag rugs and door mats. If you need it, it's here — well designed, exciting and affordable.

SHIPLEY'S. *Brevard Road at I-26. 253-1404. Mon.-Sat.* The very best in furniture and fabrics. Free design service and custom work. Woodworking and refinishing. *See discount section.*

CITIZEN'S HOME CENTER NORTH. *841 Merrimon Ave. Ph: 258-7244.* A visit upstairs to the gift deck will reveal a colorful explosion of surprises. An appealing inventory of items for kitchen, porch, patio. Quality is evident in everything - top line candles, table settings in casual styles, and clever baskets. Fun to shop especially at holiday time.

COMPLEMENTS TO THE CHEF. *374 Merrimon Ave. Ph: 258-0558.* The "Grand Old House" with everything for the kitchen. Cookware in the best of American and European designs for gourmets and gourmands.

SHOPS *
CITIZENS HOME CENTER SOUTH. *660 Hendersonville Rd. 274-0089.*
Newly expanded and perfectly beautiful garden center. Plants of
every variety for garden or interior, all accessories from hanging
baskets, to pots, plant food, garden tools and seeds. Holiday greens at
Christmas with trees, wreaths, roping and potted flowers.

BOOKSTORES
B. Dalton, Asheville Mall.
Captain's Bookshelf. Haywood St.
Asheville Bookstore. Merrimon Ave.
Baptist Book Store. Asheville Mall.
Book Trading Post. N. Lexington.
The Book Mart. Biltmore Plaza.
Beaucatcher Books. Innsbruck Mall.

FASHION *
ANTHONY'S. *Spruce Street at Thomas Wolfe Plaza, just across from
the Inn on the Plaza.* Everyone enjoys this shop and it's friendly atmosphere. Lovely clothes and exciting gift selections make the shop a
must. Excellent selection of fashionable, wearable, value oriented
sportswear. Separates, blouses and sweaters. Marvelous dresses for
many occasions. Beautiful intimate apparel corner is sophisticated yet
feminine and includes young contemporary fashions. Well selected accessories. Free parking and most credit cards accepted.
JOHN CARROLL. *39 Battery Park at Page Ave. 253-3881.* Many fashion
conscious women who enjoy elegant clothes delight in shopping this
beautiful women's store. Three floors of pure charm await the buyer.
Top name American and International designer's creations are offered
in dresses, furs, suits and lingerie. The Alley is stocked with contemporary fashions for the young and the young at heart. Shoes, sports
apparel, cosmetics, fragrances, handbags and gifts. "America's Most
Elegant Fashion Stores." *Also located 1825 N. Center St., Hickory, N.C.*
DICK SCHULMAN CO. *94 Main St., Canton, N.C. 648-4826.* Women's
better classic sportwear in natural fibers. Accessories and free alterations. A Victorian interior and coffee set a warm mood. Free UPS Service.
ENMAN'S FURRIERS. *26 Battery Park Ave. 253-0151.* Long a favorite
with Asheville and Western North Carolina shoppers looking for top
quality and high fashion in furs, jackets, short lengths, long lengths
-sport or classic and dressy. You won't be disappointed with a gift box
from Enman's.
HUNTER AND COGGINS. *566 Merrimon Ave. 252-8496.* Now Jim and
Craig bring us classic women's clothes along with fine apparel for men
that they have always carried. The best in fabrics - woolens, leathers,
natural fibers. Outfitters of distinction.
BELLS SHOPS - See Biltmore Village
JANE HABER, LTD. *40 Coxe Ave. Ph: 704/258-1512.* Absolutely
smashing costume jewelry from the Orient - cloisonne - ivory - semi-
precious stones - chains and bracelets. Jade -emerald, ruby - rings and
things at prices you'll love!

* adv.

SHOPS*

WALL STREET. This interesting old curving street in the middle of downtown is a favorite shopping stop for everyone. Some of the early architecture of Asheville is represented here. At one time Wall Street was lined with upstairs offices accessible to the street only by small bridges. In 1924 the bridges were replaced with a sidewalk. Offices have been converted to shops. Take time to browse among the small places of business. Among them are:

HIGH TEA CAFE. 23 Wall St. 255-0468. Lunch. Mon. - Fri. Tea until 5 p.m. Delicious salads, cheese plates and desserts. Best pot of tea west of London. Fresh breads. A delightful cozy spot.

THE FRUGAL FRAMER. 37 Wall St. 258-2435. 258-2435. Open all year. The center for custom framing in WNC. Area's largest and best selections of mats and moldings. The complete picture framer. Quick service.

THE YARN SPINNER. 21 Wall St. 252-1520. A business with a reputation. Over ten years of supplying serious needleworkers with everything for needlepoint, knitting and crewel. Also kits, classes and cross stitch supplies.

INSIDE LTD. 28 Wall St. 258-2630. A design shop with fine contemporary and traditional furniture at irresistable discounts. Accessories and design services. Something extravagant is waiting for you at this shop. Indulge yourself!

CAMPING

DIAMOND BRAND CAMPING CENTER, Naples, NC 28760. (704) 684-6262. US 25, Mt. Home exit from I-26. Located between Asheville and Hendersonville, Diamond Brand reflects 100 years of experience in manufacturing top quality equipment — tents, packs, light-weight sports luggage. Over 250 top name brands in camping industry. Equipment for family camping, hiking, backpacking, canoeing, climbing, cross country skiing. Technical clothes and casual sportswear. Boy Scouts - Girl Scouts uniforms and equipment. Trail guides and maps available. An outdoor specialty shop with an unusually broad selection worth seeing. *

W.N.C. FARMER'S MARKET. *570 Brevard Road off NC 191 and 1-40 and 1-26 access. 253-1691. Weekdays and Sunday afternoon. April thru December.* A marvelous new 20 acre facility operated by the North Carolina Dept. of Agriculture. The market benefits retailers, wholesalers and producers. Agriculture is a big business here, and millions of dollars are generated annually in horticultural crops. The new facility offers fresh fruits and vegetables in season, honey, sorghum molasses, plants, crafts, greens for Christmas and fresh mountain trout dipped from a tank.

LEXINGTON PARK. Corner Lexington Ave. and Walnut St. A fine example of restoration and adaptive use of some of Asheville's earliest buildings. A variety of shops and offices are filling these areas as they are restored. An old hotel has been demolished to make way for an attractive off-street parking area. Artist residents with studios open to the public are also moving into Lexington Park. People make a city come alive, and this philosophy is making a living reality of a vision.

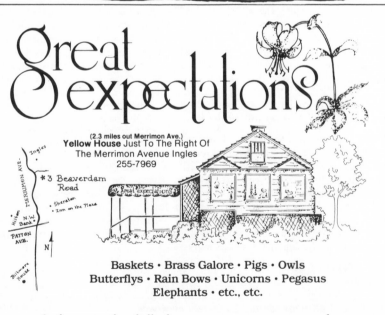

RESTAURANTS

Courtesy Asheville Chamber of Commerce   Photo - Lou Harshaw

Historic Manor Inn (C. 1890) on Charlotte St.
LISTED ON NATIONAL REGISTER OF HISTORIC PLACES

STONE SOUP RESTAURANT. *265 Charlotte St. Ph: 258-3993.*Mon.-Fri. 11 to 2. Thurs.-Sat. 5 to 8:30, Sun. 10-2. Located in the historic Manor Inn, this restaurant is a co-operative business known for its good health food. Specialties are soups, salads, sandwiches, pastries — and casseroles at night. Off expressway I-240 take Charlotte St. exit; restaurant near Grove Park Inn. *

STEVEN'S RESTAURANT AND PUB. *157 Charlotte St. Phone: 253:5348.* Daily. An elegant menu served in an intimate dining room. First time guests will be pleased and surprised at the extensive list of choices and the attentive service.

With decor created from local architectural antiques, Steven's has become one of the most popular restaurants in Western North Carolina. Lunch 11:30-2:30. Dinner from 6 p.m. The downstairs **Pub,** designed with antiques and artifacts from 1890's estate, continues to be Asheville's favorite gathering place for sophisticated locals; restaurant near Grove Park Inn.*

SHERATON MOTOR INN. *22 Woodfin St., and I-240. Ph: 253-1851.* Downtown motel with 150 rooms. Featuring the VILLAGE SQUARE RESTAURANT. Open daily 6:30 A.M. to 10:00 P.M. Special luncheon buffet on Wed.-Thurs. - Sunday. LEAN TO LOUNGE 4 P.M. to Midnight. Mon.-Sat. Rustic and relaxing. *

* adv.   47

the Peddler steak house & lounge ®

PEDDLER STEAK HOUSE. *36 Montford Ave. Asheville. Phone 704/258-0006.* Open for dinner from 5:30. Conveniently located, this new building houses the old tradition of America's favorite meal- the steak dinner. Guests can expect candlelight, music and spacious dining rooms sectioned for privacy. A steak cart brought to the table allows personal selection of size and cut for steaks cooked to order over live charcoal. Finest aged beef. Beautifully presented fruit and salad bar. The **Peddler Lounge** offers beer, wine and mixed drinks in a room complete with a handsome stone fireplace, comfortable sofas and a well appointed bar. Enjoy daily Happy Hour 5 to 7. Directions: Diagonally across from the Chamber of Commerce, take Montford Ave. exit from I-240 Expressway.*

FIREPLACE RESTAURANTS. *Two locations - 282 Smoky Park Highway W. US 19-23. Ph: 665-1146; and 330 Weaverville Hwy. N. US 25. Ph: 645-5151.* Open daily 11 A.M. to 10 P.M. Central fireplace sets the mood for these two locally owned restaurants. A menu of variety presents fine steaks, fresh seafoods, and mountain trout. Salad bar or house salad - small loaves of fresh bread served hot with every meal. Fresh vegetables in season. Luncheon menu is popular with business men and a real attraction on Sunday. Personally trained and supervised service results in excellent food at the Fireplace.*

WEAVERVILLE MILLING CO. *Reems Creek Rd. off Hwy. 25 N. or Rt. 19-23 N. Take exit at New Stock Rd. Follow signs Vance Birthplace. Ph: 645-4700.* Open everyday. Lunch Mon.-Fri. Dinner Mon.-Sat. Sunday dinner 12 to 3. This restaurant has fine continental dining in the authentic environment of a 19th century grist mill and is considered one of Buncombe County's most historic sites. Cover charge after 9 P.M. Friday and Saturday evenings for beverages and entertainment. A favorite place for residents and visitors.*

*adv.

BON APETIT AND WEINHAUS. *86-88 Patton Ave. Cafe Ph: 255-8600. Deli Ph: 254-6453.* Hours: 9-6 Closed Sunday. Fine sandwiches, homemade soups and quiche, daily specials and super salads. Extensive selection of cheeses and deli items. Croissants to take home for a heavenly breakfast. Picnic baskets assembled. Downtown Asheville near Hadley Outlet. *

ROLLIN PIN BAKERY AND COFFEE SHOP. *1000 Merrimon Ave. Ph: 253-0494.* Complete catering service and European bakery items that are superb. Many Asheville parties are planned first with a call to Rollin Pin. Coffee shop offers continental breakfast or full service breakfast, lunches or private parties arranged. *

INTERNATIONAL HOUSE OF PANCAKES RESTAURANT

251 Tunnel Road at Junction of U.S. 70 and U.S. 74, I-240 - Tunnel Road Exit. 255-8601.

Daily from 6:30 a.m. Best place for breakfast and a great place for lunch and dinner–specialty of the house consists of 17 varieties of pancakes. Also waffles and dessert crepes. Super sandwiches. Any menu items may be ordered to take out. Of special interest to foreign visitors is the weinerwald European roast chicken, served daily from 4:00 p.m. Ample parking. Near Asheville Mall. *

1501 PATTON AVENUE — ASHEVILLE, N.C.
PHONE 258-1198

A FAMILY RESTAURANT

THE FISHOUSE, *1501 Patton Avenue. U.S. 19-23 southwest of Asheville. (704) 258-1198.* Open all year. Wed.-Sat. 4:30 p.m.-9 p.m. Sunday 12 p.m.-9 p.m. This is the original fish house in Asheville. Excellent fresh seafood cooked and served Calabash style (Calabash refers to a North Carolina coastal town famous for its many seafood restaurants). The Fishouse is a 250 seat family style restaurant. Plain good food, good prices.

NEW FISHOUSE. *Second location. Oak Ridge Highway, Knoxville, Tennessee (615) 584-6816.* Open Tuesday through Sunday. *

THE COACH LITE. *Long Shoals Road. Skyland Exit from I-26 and NC 280 South. Ph: 684-3137.* BUFFET LUNCH from 11:30 and dinners Mon.-Sat. from 5:30. Music Tues.-Fri. Prime ribs (under $10.00) - steaks - fresh seafoods - chicken. Casual and friendly and worth the twenty minute drive from Asheville or Hendersonville. Closed Sunday. *

RODEWAY INN®

RODEWAY INN. *Located East of Asheville between Oteen and Swannanoa on U.S. 70. Exit 55 from I-40. (704) 298-7952.* Rodeway has a full service restaurant; the popular Sunday Buffet Lunch features a bountiful, well-planned menu. CINCLAIR'S at Rodeway is a lively night spot with top entertainment and a large dance floor. Beer, wine and set-ups. No cover charge Monday and Tuesday. Open until after midnight every night all year. **Rodeway Accommodations:** 122 rooms featuring Satellite TV and HBO. *

GROSVENORS. *Inn on the Plaza. 252-8211.* The shimmering view of the mountains from this roof top restaurant is rivaled only by the quality and service offered. Live evening entertainment.

AUNT MINNIE'S WISDOM. *Great Smokies Hilton. 254-3211.* Delightful food-decor-service. A pleasant stop for lunch or dinner.

GROVE PARK INN. *290 Macon Ave. 252-2711.* Plantation Dining Room, handsome lobby bar or Sunset Terrace with its beautiful view.

GATSBY'S. *13 Walnut St., 254-4248.* Gourmet salads and sandwiches, beautiful hand built bar and outside dining available. Mon.-Sat. 11-11, Fri.-Sat. 11 to late with live entertainment. Downtown Asheville.

DEERPARK. *Biltmore House Grounds 274-1776.* Lunch daily for Biltmore House visitors. Private group luncheons and dinners also. April-October.

PISGAH INN. *South on Blue Ridge Parkway, 20 miles from Asheville. 235-8228.* May through Oct. Full service restaurant at over 5,000 feet. Also coffee shop. A special treat.

ETHNIC RESTAURANTS
French
Jared's. 60 Haywood. Ph: 252-8276.
Market Place. 10 N. Market St. Ph: 252-4162.
Italian
Piccolo Mondo. 23 Page Ave. Ph: 255-0413.
Iron Gate. 2. S. Tunnel Rd. Ph: 298-5773.
Chinese
Ming Tree. S. Tunnel Rd. K-Mart Plaza. Ph: 298-4839.
Fang's. 579 Tunnel Rd. Ph: 298-1800.
Mexican
Poncho's La Casita. S. Tunnel Rd. 298-2578.
Fiesta Cantina. 2 Regent Park at Smoky Park Bridge. Ph: 252-3314.
Greek
Three Brothers, 183 Haywood Rd. Ph: 253-4971.
Mountaineer Steak House. 148 S. Tunnel Rd. Ph: 254-3332.

* adv.

BLACK MOUNTAIN — SWANNANOA
MONTREAT — RIDGECREST
(US 70—I-40—NC 9)

The "Valley" refers to that lovely stretch of land on the Western side of the Blue Ridge, cradled by the Swannanoa Mountains on one side and the great Craggies and Old Gray Beard on the other. In the distance looms the dark heights of the Black Mountains. This area is rich in history and it is the largest Religious Conference Center in the world. The town of Black Mountain was first called Gray Eagle. In the late 1870's the railroad built the longest of seven tunnels (1800 feet) bringing trains up the mountain from Old Fort to Asheville. Hikers arriving by train would ask to be put off at the Black Mountain stop, so the original name was changed. *Elevation is 2400 feet in town and surrounding mountains range up to 6100 feet. Mt. Mitchell (6,684 feet) is in the Black Mountains.*

RELIGIOUS CONFERENCE CENTERS

RIDGECREST. *US 70 east of Black Mountain. 669-8022.* Baptist conference center. Open all year. Largest in the south. Owned and operated by the Southern Baptist Convention. At least 56,000 people attend this conference center each year. Baptist Book Store on grounds.

MONTREAT. *NC 9 North off US 70.* Conference center of the Presbyterian Church, U.S., Montreat is a residential community and college campus (*Montreat-Anderson*). Mountain beauty, streams, lake, swimming pool, shops. Turn at stop light center of Black Mountain. Assembly Inn - 669-8441. Dining room open to public serving all meals daily.

BLUE RIDGE ASSEMBLY. *US 70 Black Mountain, 669-8422.* Founded in 1906 as a conference and leadership training center. Blue Ridge Assembly is owned and operated by the Y.M.C.A.'s of the ten southeastern states. This four season conference center is in a magnificent setting.

CHRISTMONT CHRISTIAN ASSEMBLY. *NC 9, south of Black Mountain. 669-8977.* Run by the Christian Church (Disciples of Christ). The 640 acre property was acquired from the estate of Raphael Guastavino, Spanish architect who worked six years on the Biltmore House and built the dome of St. Lawrence Church in Asheville. Guastavino fired his tiles in a kiln that has been preserved on the property. Hiking trails and over 5,000 varieties of wild flowers.

IN THE OAKS EPISCOPAL CONFERENCE CENTER. *Vance Ave. (704) 669-2117.* Owned by Episcopal Diocese of WNC. Operated year round. Conferences and small meetings. Indoor swimming pool, gym.

MONTE VISTA HOTEL. *US 70 (704) 699-2119.* Open year round. Owned by the Phillips family since 1919, this comfortable hotel has long been a favorite of conference goers and summer residents. Sixty-seven rooms with a new first floor addition. Serving all meals except Sunday evening. Popular after church Sunday buffet.*

OTHER RESTAURANTS include the COACH HOUSE, *US 70; OLYMPIA, US 70 East.* OLDE HOUSE RESTAURANT. *US 70 Ridgecrest (704) 669-8354.*

*adv.   51

BLACK MOUNTAIN SHOPS

GIFT CRAFTS. *114 W. State St., May-Dec. 669-8217.* Small shop but big on crafts carefully selected with taste and emphasis on Mother Nature. Pottery is the specialty. Also wood and woven items.*

CHERRY STREET has a variety of small shops appealing to every interest.*

LAUER'S ANTIQUES. *100 Cherry St., 669-2080. Summer.* "Antiques and other elderly things" are pleasantly displayed for collectors of furniture, china, silver, jewelry and oriental objects. Depression glass.

ANNE'S CALICO CORNER. *105 Cherry St., 669-9107. Open year round.* Calico, ginghams and country prints. Quilting supplies. Craft classes, handmade gifts, alterations. Stop in, have coffee and share an idea.

A TOUCH OF GLASS. *137 Cherry St.* Traveling through space 39,000,000 miles in 8 minutes, light shines upon us. Come by this shop and let them capture your light and the ramblings of your mind in stained glass. Or call 669-2069.

BLACK-EYED SUSAN DELI. *126 Cherry St., Black Mountain, N.C. and Montreat. (behind the Post Office)* Kosher Meats, N.Y. Cheese Cake, Pocket Bread, Salads, Soups, Cold Plates. Catering for all occasions. *669-2817. Mon.-Sat.: 11:00-3:00.*

OLD DEPOT ASSOCIATION ARTS AND CRAFTS CENTER. *Sutton St. 669-6583. One block south of US 70.* Artists from the Swannanoa Valley bring paintings and crafts for sale. *Closed for winter months.*

THE GRAY EAGLE GIFT SHOP. *101 Broadway. 669-8734. Open all year.* For that special "take home" gift. North Carolina books.

APRONS BY CLAUDIA McGRAW. *203 E. State St., US 70. 669-2363.* Claudia's fame has spread, but all of her Black Mountain neighbors have known her beautiful aprons since 1932. Custom orders.

Archeological Dig - Warren Wilson College   *Courtesy - Warren Wilson College*

WARREN WILSON COLLEGE
Swannanoa, North Carolina 28778

Founded in 1894 as the Asheville Farm School and merging with Dorland Bell School to become a two year college in 1942, Warren Wilson College has been a four year liberal arts college since 1965. It is covenant related to the Synod of the South, United Presbyterian Church. With an enrollment of 496 students, young men and women come from 38 states and 23 overseas nations. The Bachelor of Arts degree is offered in 18 majors. Independent study and interdisciplinary courses and majors are available. Ph: 704/298-3325.

Crowfields
CONDOMINIUMS

A prestigious community located at 1745 Hendersonville Road, just 6 miles south of downtown Asheville.
Models open weekdays 9 to 5, weekends 1-5 or by appointment.
274-0179

another quality achievement of Beverly-Grant, Inc.

BILTMORE HOUSE AND GARDENS
Registered National Historic Landmark
Asheville, North Carolina.

*Open all year except Thanksgiving, Christmas and New Year's Day. Open
9 A.M. to 5 P.M. (privately owned)*

Directions: *On U.S. 25, 3 blocks north of I-40 Exit 50 or 50B in
South Asheville.*

BILTMORE HOUSE *(1895)*

HISTORY: Construction was started in 1890 and Biltmore House was formally opened at a Christmas party in 1895. George Washington Vanderbilt was the grandson of Commodore Cornelius Vanderbilt of the New York Central Railroad. Young Mr. Vanderbilt visited Asheville in the late 1880's with his mother. Impressed with the splendor of the mountain scenery, the lush growth of the forests and the temperate climate, he acquired the land to fulfill his dream of the finest country house in America.

55

BILTMORE HOUSE AND GARDENS (con't)

Mr. Vanderbilt purchased 125,000 acres, including farms, forests, and the small village of Best which is now Biltmore. The land was selected for its perfect location overlooking and including the confluence of the French Broad and Swannanoa Rivers. Designed by Richard Morris Hunt, America's foremost exponent of French Renaissance architecture, Biltmore House emerged as a French Chateau with opulence and elegance unequalled in America, and unexpected in the mountains of Western North Carolina.

Two men were responsible for the magnificent landscaping of the estate. Frederic Law Olmsted, noted for his design of new York's Central Park, created the original plan for the estate's landscaping. After his death, a Canadian landscape architect, Chauncey Delos Beadle, executed Mr. Olmsted's plans. The Estate's acres of azaleas are perfectly maintained along streams, walkways, and formal gardens.

During World War II Biltmore House provided safe storage for priceless works of art from the National Gallery of Art in Washington, D.C. Protection was maintained by 24-hour armed guards, and the storage area was the west room of the main floor. The west room was not completed in Mr. Vanderbilt's lifetime, and in 1976, after extensive remodeling, the room was opened to the public for the first time. The major rooms with original furniture and paintings are shown in this 255 room castle. After Mr. Vanderbilt's death in 1914, a large portion of the estate was deeded to the U.S. Government to form the nucleus of the Pisgah National Forest which lies southwest of Asheville.

Part of the original land of the Estate was incorporated into the residential town of Biltmore Forest, and later part of the land was sold for a portion of the Blue Ridge Parkway. Interstate highways I-26 and I-40 cross the property but do not mar the serenity and quiet feeling of the 12,000 acre estate. Two self-guided tours of Biltmore House are available. The "Upstairs Tour" is comprised of 22 of the mansion's more formal rooms and areas on the first and second floors, including the Palm Court, Billiard Room, Banquet Hall, Family Dining Room, Music Room, Tapestry Gallery, Library and Family Guest Bedrooms. Opened in 1980, the "Downstairs Tour" depicts the other side of life at Biltmore House and includes the Laundries, Kitchens, Pantries, Servants Quarters, Gymnasium, Swimming Pool and Bowling Alley. The two tours may be purchased separately or in combination. Both tours include the gardens. Children under 12 are admitted free of charge when accompanied by parent.

Don't miss the Celebration of Christmas at Biltmore House. The annual Christmas festivities follow the grand tradition of the late 1880's Seasonal trees, garlands, poinsettias, fruits and candles adorn the house. Special musical programs are held each weekend in December. This should be a part of your Christmas holiday!

AMBASSADOR PASS TO BILTMORE HOUSE. Ask ticket seller for you Ambassador pass. After your first paid visit each season, this pass entitles you to a free tour each time you bring one or more paying visitors to Biltmore House and Gardens.

Christmas at Biltmore House

DEERPARK RESTAURANT. Deerpark Restaurant on Biltmore's grounds is part of a series of handsome English-style buildings designed by Richard Morris Hunt, Biltmore's original architect, in the 1890's for Biltmore Estate's farm operations. Originally a dairy barn, Deerpark has been renovated into a unique, open-air restaurant with seating for up to 500 people around a beautifully landscaped courtyard. Deerpark is open to Biltmore House visitors for lunch daily from mid-April to October 31. Deerpark is also available for private group luncheons and dinners. For banquet menus, prices and reservation procedures call or write: *The Biltmore Company, Marketing Department, One Biltmore Plaza, Asheville, N.C. 28803. 704/274-1776.*

All Souls Church, Biltmore, N. C.

ALL SOULS CHURCH

BILTMORE, N.C.

Consecrated in 1896, All Souls Episcopal Church was designed by Richard M. Hunt, architect of Biltmore House. The design of the church was inspired by churches in the Cumberland district of Northern England. A gothic style of the transitional period from Norman to Romanesque, it is built in cruciform like a small cathedral. The first weather vane on the tower was a cock which was replaced later by St. Hubert's stag with a cross between the antlers. The weather vane you see today symbolizes a beautiful cross encircling the world, and it was designed and executed by Marianne Zabriskie, wife of the present rector.

BILTMORE VILLAGE

All Soul's Church was the focal point for a model village which was planned by George Vanderbilt and executed by architects Richard M. Hunt, Richard S. Smith and landscape architect Frederick L. Olmstead. Constructed at the turn of the century, the village houses were designed to accommodate employees and staff required to operate the large estate of Biltmore. For over sixty years the cottages in Biltmore Village were private homes. During the 1970's the village underwent extensive renovation and a group of small shops opened- GIFTS, CRAFTS, AND WEARING APPAREL. Biltmore Village has been declared an historic area. You will enjoy browsing in the small shops on All Soul's Crescent, Boston Way and Swan Street.

BILTMORE VILLAGE
HISTORIC DISTRICT

A charming community of shops and galleries

BILTMORE VILLAGE INNE, 5 *Boston Way.* 274-4100. Open all year. Charming restaurant with colonial atmosphere. Natural ingredients in traditional southern dishes. A fine variety of meats, seafood and fruits. The proprietors pride themselves in serving elegant food. Dining inside or outside on covered deck or open patio. Fine wines, beers and mixed drinks. Lunch, Tea and Dinner served. Suggest reservations during tourist season. Strolling musicians on weekends. *Closed Sundays.* *

MUDPIES, 1 *Swan Street,* 274-2678. A shop for children and a "must" for grandmothers. Beautiful clothes and accessories for infant girls to size 14 and infant boys to size 7. Special gifts for special seasons. Two floors to shop in this historic house. *

VILLAGE GALLERIES. 9 *Boston Way.* 274-2424. Area's largest supply of original graphics, etchings, lithographs, silkscreens, Japanese woodblock prints, watercolors and limited edition prints. Quality custom framing. Conveniently located near Biltmore House entrance.*

B. TAYLOR. 3 *Biltmore Plaza.* Don't fail to visit this stylish shop! Clothes completely feminine. Better dresses and separates. Gorgeous fabrics and color. Sizes 4 to 14. In the building with Fireside Antiques.*

THE VILLAGE ART & CRAFT FAIR

Held annually on the grounds of All Souls Church. Sponsored by the New Morning Gallery, the daytime fair takes place on the same August weekend as the Annual Dance and Folk Festival. (See Civic Center, Asheville.)

Bell's Traditionals, Ltd. *

BELL'S TRADITIONALS LTD. *Kitchen Place, Biltmore Village. 274-2630. Open all year. Closed Sundays.* Bell's has a corner on the clothes market with a collection of unusual shops. Bell's Executive Shop, Carriage Shop, Village Manor and College Corner are outstanding fashion shops for quality conscious men, women and boys. You will recognize outstanding brand names such as Southwick, Norman Hilton, Corbin, Deansgate for men, and Gordon of Philadelphia, Austin Hill, E.S. Deans, Leon Levin, Jerry Silverman and Victor Costa for women. Enjoy the whole scene, complete with the old timey marble drugstore fountain still in use for cokes while you shop in Bell's Shop for Pappagallo.

BELL'S OUTDOOR OUTFITTERS. *One Boston Way. 274-2630.* Speciality shop for anyone who enjoys backpacking and technical rock climbing. Representing Wilderness Experience, Sierra Designs, Woolrich, Lowe, Old Town, etc. The outdoor equipment is for backpacking, camping, cross country skiing, canoeing, kayaking. Good looking functional outdoor clothing for the entire family.

BELL'S GATEHOUSE GIFTS AND ANTIQUES. *Entrance to Biltmore Estate, 274-2465. Open all year. Seven days.* An atmosphere of unique and unusual gifts. Great variety in decorative accessories, with gifts in pewter, brass, china and crystal. Framed and unframed limited edition prints. Antiques. A shop that boasts: "Something for everybody."

Photo - Fireside Antiques

FIRESIDE ANTIQUES. *Five Biltmore Plaza. 274-5977. Open all year.* Direct importers of European antiques. This shop reflects three generations of taste and appreciation. Fine architectural details enhance the handsome eighteenth and nineteenth century European furniture as well as American antiques and some choice reproductions. Design consultation by appointment. *Parent Shop: Cleveland, Mississippi.* *

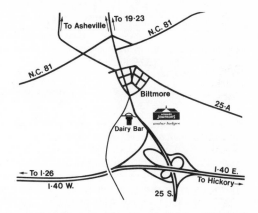

DAIRY FARMS, INC.
ASHEVILLE, NORTH CAROLINA

BILTMORE DAIRY BAR. *Corner Hendersonville Road (U.S. 25) and Vanderbilt Road. 274-2370. Open 7 days a week, all year except Christmas and New Year's Day.* Serving a hearty breakfast from 7 a.m., the Dairy Bar is an Asheville tradition. Residents and visitors stop regularly for lunch and ice cream treats. Sandwiches, salads and homemade soups are always good with plenty of dairy fresh desserts. Thousands of children have enjoyed the ice cream combinations that are concocted for pure eye-popping pleasure! King of the Fountain is a specialty with eight scoops of ice cream and a variety of surprises in one dish! Biltmore Dairy Farms Premium All Natural Ice Cream is smooth, rich and healthful, blended with loving care and 80 years experience.   Plant and main offices are located in Asheville.   Other dairy bars: Brevard and Waynesville. *

MOTELS NEAR BILTMORE HOUSE

HOWARD JOHNSON'S MOTOR LODGE. *190 Hendersonville Road, U.S. 25 South of Asheville, Exit U.S. 25 - Biltmore Estate from I-40. (704) 274-2300. Toll free reservations (1-800) 654-2000.* Offering comfort and personal attention, Asheville's Howard Johnson's is a 68 room motel with king-size beds, special suites, all conveniences, family swimming pool and restaurant. Open 24 hours. Located near Biltmore House entrance and Biltmore Village. *

FOREST MANOR MOTOR LODGE. *866 Hendersonville Road, U.S. 25. 274-3531.* Located opposite Biltmore Forest on U.S. 25 south of Asheville, this 21 unit motel is beautifully landscaped amid five acres of tall pines and informal flower gardens. A family run motel, look for cheerful cottages. King-size beds, color TV, air conditioning. No smoking rooms available. Near Biltmore House, Blue Ridge Parkway and Asheville Hendersonville Airport. *

BUENA VISTA MOTEL. *1080 Hendersonville Road (704) 274-1646.* Open all year. Twenty-three units including 4 kitchen units. Small, family motel. Clean, comfortable accommodations. Cable TV. Convenient location for Blue Ridge Parkway and area shopping and sightseeing. Located U.S. 25, 2 miles south of Biltmore. Take U.S. 25 south exit from I-40. *

CHEROKEE COUNTY
Established 1839

COUNTY SEAT: *Murphy*
ELEVATION: *1,535 Ft.*
POPULATION: *18,933*

The county was named for the Cherokee Indians, some of whom still live in the area. In 1830 the first white settlers came into Cherokee County Principal Towns: Murphy, Andrews, Brasstown.

In 1838 all but a few refugee Indians were removed from Fort Butler, Murphy and Fort Delaney, Andrews, and were forced to march under guard along the "Trail of Tears" to Oklahoma. The Cherokee people left behind their legends, mountains, and heritage. By 1840, over 3,000 people had built homes and were farming the valleys. One hundred years later the coming of the Tennessee Valley Authority and the huge lake system brought many changes to the area. Today, 20,000 people are engaged in farming and industry. Lakes Hiwassee and Appalachia, covering 8,000 acres offer unspoiled environmental pleasure. Tourists come for boating and fishing. The county has 30 or more trout streams and park facilities for campers, hikers and nature lovers. Cherokee County Chamber of Commerce, Murphy, NC 28906 (704) 837-2242.

MURPHY
U.S. 19-23 7 U.S. 64 S.W., near Georgia line.

THE WALKER INN dates from 1840 and was owned by Indian Chief Junaluska, who served with General Andrew Jackson and was famed for his courage and bravery. Originally a small log structure, Walker Inn was expanded to its present size by 1864. The interior has been unaltered since the nineteenth century. Original features still intact include iron hinges, bubble glass, beamed ceilings and old door latches. Following the Civil War and before the railroad was built, a stage coach run from Murphy to Franklin made regular stops at Walker's Inn for overnight stays. Many travelers and scientists came to see the beautiful wild country. The house is open by appointment, 10 AM to 5 PM April through October. No charge.

The Espicopal Church of the Messiah. Murphy. Organized in 1855 and cornerstone laid in 1896. Heart pine paneling is laid in herringbone pattern. The altar was handmade and the glass windows were executed by Tiffany's of New York.

Fields of the Woods. Hwy 294, near Murphy. A Biblical Wonder of sculptures and monuments depicting Biblical symbols. A 150 feet long and 115 feet wide cross sits atop All Nations Mountain (El. 2210). Many other replicas in giant structures.

The Mountain Emporium. Main St., Andrews, N. C. A sheltered workshop providing employment for handicapped adults and operated by Industrial Opportunities, Inc. Custom ordered furniture, children's corner with toys, and crafts. Most credit cards accepted.

SMOKY MOUNTAIN ARTS AND CRAFTS SHOW. Held every year over the 4th of July weekend. Only indoor exhibit in the area, it presents artist from the Southern Appalachian Mountains.

Cherokee County Historical Museum. Murphy, N. C. A large collection of Indian artifacts, Early American housewares, "Fairy Crosses" and other minerals, firearms and old musical instruments. Special exhibits offer a comprehensive study in local history. The collection was made available to the Museum by Mr. Herman H. West. Open Monday through Friday- 9-5. Saturday, 10-2. No charge.

CAMPBELL FOLK SCHOOL. *Brasstown, N.C. (Near Murphy) (704) 837-2775.* Instruction, rest and relaxation have been a successful combination for fifty years at the Campbell Folk School. The woodsy campus is alive with opportunities to experience the outstanding features of our folk heritage. The Brasstown carvers have achieved wide recognition. Wood carving and furniture construction are courses that are emphasized. Others are offered in iron work, pottery, weaving, leatherwork, quilting, macrame, batik and jewelry making. Folk dancing and music are performed and taught throughout the weeks of school. Prominent guest instructors spend part of their summers at Brasstown. For information on program and college credit write: *Campbell Folk School, Dept. A, Brasstown, N.C.*

RESTAURANT — SHOPPING

OAK BARREL. *Old County Home. U.S. 19-19A, about one mile from Murphy.* What a fine idea to make this old establishment into a well run restaurant.

CRAFT SHOP. *Mt. Folk Center, U.S. 64 West.* A Cherokee County cooperative that is Federally sponsored and non-profit. Authentic handmade crafts.
BRUMBY TEXTILE MILLS OUTLET. *Tennessee St.* T shirts for men - shirts are sold from the plant (not a shop). Very inexpensive and very good buys.

ACCOMMODATIONS:
Bear Paw. Rt. 4, Murphy, N. C. Phone: 644-5451.

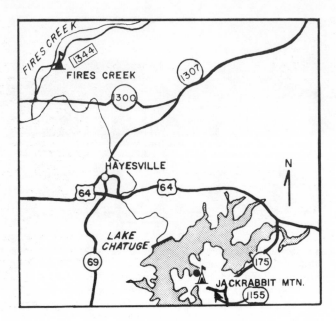

CLAY COUNTY
Established 1861

COUNTY SEAT:, HAYESVILLE, *Elevation 1,893 Ft.*
COUNTY POPULATION: *6,619*
PRINCIPAL PLACES: *Lake Chatuge, Jackrabbit Mountain, Hayesville, Chatuge Dam*

Clay County is the most sparsely populated of all the mountain counties and is an ideal place to "get away from it all." Here, the Appalachian Trail winds through scenic mountains covered with wild azaleas, laurel, pine, dogwod, and white and red oak. One hundred thirty-one shore miles of Lake Chatuge are in Clay County, and fishing, swimming, boating, and water skiing can all be enjoyed in its cool, clear waters. Breathtaking mountain scenery is everywhere - 64,241 acres of the Nantahala National Forest are in Clay County - along with a ninety year old court house in the picturesque county seat of Hayesville. Clay County was named in honor of statesman Henry Clay.

JACKRABBIT MOUNTAIN. *U.S. 64 east of Hayesville; turn right on N.C. 175; right on N.C. 1155.* Developed campground on 6,950-acre Lake Chatuge. Swimming, boating, hiking, fishing, amphitheater.

CHATUGE SHORES GOLF COURSE. NC 69 - *(704) 389-8940.*
SHEWBIRD MOUNTAIN LODGE. Off US 69 - *(704) 389-8925.* Rooms, cottages.

Upper Falls   Snowbird Creek   *Courtesy - U. S. Forest Service Photo*

GRAHAM COUNTY
Established 1872

COUNTY SEAT: ROBBINSVILLE. *Elevation 2,150 feet*
COUNTY POPULATION: *7,217*
PRINCIPAL PLACES: *Robbinsville, Fontana Lake and Village*

The county was named for William A. Graham, Governor of North Carolina. Containing over 112,000 acres of the Nantahala National Forest, the county is 60% forest land. Oak, chestnut, hemlock and poplar abound. There are nine communities and two schools in the county. Tourism is one of the major industries and trout fishing is found in numerous fresh water streams. There are three large lakes - Fontana - Cheoah - Santeetlah - lake fishing is good also. Hunters will note that Graham County has a population of black bear, wild Russian boar, and white-tailed deer along with small game. Joyce Kilmer Forest has many trails for hiking through virgin timber. Chief Junaluska's grave is within the city limits of the town of Robbinsville, and the famous Appalachian Trail goes through a portion of the county. There are many motels and campgrounds in Graham County.

For more information:
  Cheoah Ranger District
  District Ranger
  U.S. Forest Service
  Route 1, Box 16-A - U.S. 129 north of Robbinsville
  Robbinsville, N.C. 28771
  (704) 479-6431

BLUE BOAR LODGE. *Joyce Kilmer Forest Road. Off U.S. 129 north of Robbinsville. (704) 479-8126.* Summer season May 1 through Sept. 30. Small rustic lodge with accommodations for 16 guests. Built in 1950 as a hunting lodge, Blue Boar continues the tradition with a boar hunting season, mid October through end of December. Dining room serves three meals a day, family style. Good southern, home cooking. Lodge has access to Santeetlah Lake. Boat dock, swimming and boats for rent. Stocked trout pond on property. Guests may fish for dinner! *

SNOWBIRD MOUNTAIN LODGE: *Robbinsville, N.C. 28771.*

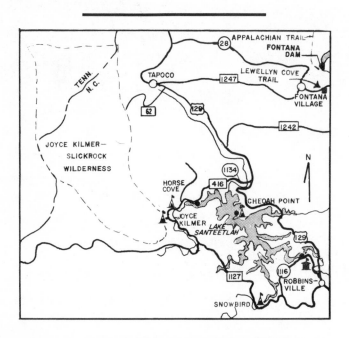

NANTAHALA NATIONAL FOREST RECREATION AREAS

CABLE COVE. *N.C. 28 east of Fontana Lake. Turn left on Forest Service Road 520.* Developed campground, boating, fishing, water skiing, nature trail, and boat ramp.

HORSE COVE. *U.S. 129 north of Robbinsville.* Along mountain stream; near Joyce Kilmer-Slickrock Wilderness and Santeetlah Lake. Developed campground, hiking, boating, and fishing.

SNOWBIRD. *U.S. 129 north of Robbinsville.* Developed picnic area on Snowbird Creek.

JOYCE KILMER-SLICKROCK WILDERNESS. *U.S. 129 north of Robbinsville.* 15,000 acre wilderness with mountain streams. 3,800 acre virgin forest. Developed picnic area, hiking, fishing and hunting.

CHEOAH POINT. *U.S. 129 north of Robbinsville.* On Lake Santeetlah. Developed campground.

FONTANA VILLAGE RESORT

Fontana Lodge

Courtesy -
Fontana Village Resort

RESORTS AND LODGES:

FONTANA VILLAGE RESORT.* *Fontana Dam, N.C. (704) 498-2211. Between U.S. 129 and U.S. 19.* A complete family resort with Inn and Cottages. Wide variety of recreation in the perfect location for a mountain vacation. Situated at the southeastern edge of the Great Smoky Mountains National Park, near Fontana and Cheoah Lakes, the Appalachian Trail and the Nantahala National Forest. *65 miles from Knoxville, TN and 95 miles west of Asheville, N.C.*

FONTANA VILLAGE INN. Open all year. 94 rooms. Opened in 1975 with all luxuries. Comfortable rooms, color TV, saunas, swimming pool. PIONEER ROOM, a full service restaurant with gourmet dining, appeals to the most discriminating taste. CAFETERIA - open to the public.

COTTAGES - 275 housekeeping units - one to three bedrooms with modern furnishings. In park setting with mountain stream, trails and bridges.

Other Fontana features include trout pond (no license required), shuffleboard, Fontana School of Art, Nature Program, tennis, swimming, and the highlight of Fontana's recreation program— SQUARE DANCING: Five annual world famous dance festivals and Appalachian style square dancing open to all comers three nights a week. You will agree that Fontana is the "square dance capitol of the world."

Also at Fontana: VILLAGE GREEN, shopping center. Five tennis courts lighted for night play.

FONTANA SWIMMING POOL. Located between village and top of dam, olympic size. Also wading pool for children. Picnic area. Snack bar. Lifeguard. Open June till Labor Day.

FONTANA GOLF COURSE. Nine hole course.

FONTANA MARINA. All supplies and boats for fishing and water sports on Fontana Lake. Service station, food market, 4 gift shops, crafts work shop, playground, movie theater. Riding stables.

Fontana Village has everything you need for a perfect family vacation.

*adv.

HAYWOOD COUNTY
Established 1808

COUNTY SEAT: WAYNESVILLE, *elevation 2,635* ft.
COUNTY POPULATION: *46,495*
PRINCIPAL PLACES: *Waynesville, Lake Junaluska, Maggie Valley, Hazelwood, Canton, Clyde*

Haywood County was named in honor of John Haywood, Treasurer of North Carolina, 1787-1827. Considering itself the "Vacation Center" of the Great Smoky Mountains, Haywood County has much to offer the visitor. High mountains, superb climate, beautiful scenery, sparkling waters, historical sites, planned recreation, good roads, and much more beckon the vacationer. A balanced economy is supported by industry and agriculture; there are four major industries and several diversified manufacturers. Haywood County is the gateway to the Great Smoky Mountain National Park, and the Blue Ridge Parkway traverses its southern border. Most major tourist attractions are within an easy drive. The highest elevations on the Blue Ridge Parkway are in Haywood County. There are also over 68,000 acres of the Pisgah National Forest.

EARLY HISTORY: All of Haywood County originally was part of the Cherokee Indian Nation. After the end of the Revolutionary War, a great number of English, Scotch-Irish, German and Dutch settlers made their way into the area. At this time, the Cherokees gave up much of their land and moved west to the Tuckasegee River. The formation of the county, from Buncombe, was completed in March, 1809. Waynesville, originally known as Mount Prospect, is the County Seat.

Haywood County Chamber of Commerce, Waynesville, NC 28786, Phone (704) 456-3021.

LAKE JUNALUSKA
U.S. 19-23 - I-40.

LAKE JUNALUSKA METHODIST ASSEMBLY. A year round conference center situated on a 250 acre lake, this assembly is an extensive educational, recreational and religious facility for the Methodist Church. **The Terrace and The Colonial** offer accommodations to conference goers. There is an outstanding historical exhibit in the World Methodist Building that is open to the public. Behind the building are the Susanne Wesley Gardens - a favorite place for weddings. The Rose Walk, planted along the lake, has numerous varieties and is in bloom all summer. The Memorial Chapel and Stuart Auditorium events are open to the public. Cokesbury Bookstore is also in the complex.*HISTORY NOTE: Bishop Francis Asbury, a circuit rider in the early 1800's, spread the Methodist influence and traveled nearly 228,000 miles carrying his message to cabins and roadside gatherings. In the Beaverdam section of Asheville, a large rock under a huge oak tree was his pulpit. The rock remains as a simple memorial to his work.*

PISGAH NATIONAL FOREST RECREATION AREAS:

SHINING ROCK WILDERNESS. *Blue Ridge Parkway milepost 420.* Hiking, fishing. 13,400-acre area preserved in its primary state. Waterfalls, steep rock slopes, mountain streams. Entrance permit required.

SUNBURST RECREATION AREA. *U.S. 276 east of Waynesville. N.C. 215.*

WAYNESVILLE
West of Asheville U.S. 19-23 and I-40

ANNUAL EVENTS
Ramp Race and Festival - Early May, Waynesville.
Antique Car Show - Late June, Maggie Valley.
Boosters Fireworks and Carnival - July 4th., Waynesville.
Smoky Mountain Folk Festival - Late July, Waynesville.
Cataloochee Trail Ride - Late May, early June, late September, Maggie Valley.
Canton Labor Day Celebration - Sept., Canton.
Haywood County Farm Festival - Late September, Canton.
Lake Junaluska Road Race - Early October, Lake Junaluska.
Maggie Valley Arts and Crafts Show - Late October, Maggie Valley.

The Shelton House
SHELTON HOUSE
Listed in National Register of Historic Places
THE MUSEUM OF NORTH CAROLINA HANDICRAFTS, *Pigeon and Shelton Streets, Waynesville, N. C. (704) 452-1551.* Situated on a spacious, tree-shaded lot, the Shelton House recalls rural origins and stands as a prominent representative of late 19th century agrarian prosperity in Haywood County. The spacious two story frame house has a two-tier porch and bracketed eves. it was constructed between 1876 and 1880 for Stephen Jehu Shelton (1835-1913), a Confederate officer and veteran. The Museum was opened in August 1980, and handicrafts have been given or are on loan by master craftsmen from all sections of the state. Many items are also from pioneer days. Open May 1-Nov. 1; Wed.-Sat. 10-5; Sun. 2-5.

SHOPS
HALE'S - *131 North Main St., Waynesville, NC (704) 456-6069.* Hale's has been a Waynesville tradition for nearly 60 years, attracting customers from other towns and states. You will find exclusive clothes from designers such as Vera Maxwell, Mollie Parnis, Abe Schrader, Jerry Silverman and Earnest Strauss. Stunning sport clothes and better dresses. *
THE GENERAL STORE - *22 Howell Mill Rd., U.S. 276 S exit from 19A-23 Bypass, (704) 456-7858.* Authentic, hand hewn log cabins full of local crafts, primitive antiques and country pieces; wooden things, pottery, leather. A very popular stop in the Waynesville area. *

MAGGIE VALLEY
U.S. 19, 35 miles West of Asheville

Maggie Valley is a small resort and retirement community, nestled in the mountains "Where spring spends the summer and lingers through the fall". Because thousands of vacationers enter the Great Smoky Mountains National Park by U.S. 19, Maggie Valley is appropriately called the gateway to the Smokies. Maggie offers a variety of amusements including Ghost Town, the Maggie Valley golf course, Soco Gardens and Zoo, many craft shops and restaurants. You will find a Holiday Inn as well as lodging in privately owned cottages and cabins. For more information write: Maggie Valley Chamber of Commerce, P. O. Box 87, Maggie Valley NC 28751 (704) 926-1686

MAGGIE VALLEY, N.C.
U.S. 19 AND 23

Season: Early May to Late October 9 a.m. to 6 p.m.

WESTERN GHOST TOWN	MUSICAL REVIEW
INCLINE RAILWAY	LIVE COUNTRY MUSIC
CHAIR LIFT	MINING TOWN CRAFTS AND GIFT SHOPS
GUN FIGHTS	AMERICAN HIGH DIVING CHAMPIONS
SALOON SHOWS	COMEDIAN - VENTRILOQUIST
GAMES - ARCADE	PICNIC FACILITIES
PONY AND TRAIL RIDES	RESTAURANTS

RON URBAN'S INTERNATIONAL ICE SHOW

35 miles from Asheville   45 miles from Gatlinburg, Tenn.
95 miles from Knoxville, Tenn.

HAYWOOD COUNTY RESTAURANTS:

MOUNTAIN VIEW CAFETERIA - *US 19, Maggie Valley. Open daily Mid-April-October 31.* A family business for 20 years. Great reputation and great food. Country cooking. Roast beef, ham, chicken and fish. Fresh vegetables and homemade breads and desserts. Very popular. Reasonable prices. *

Heath Lodge - 900 Dolan Road.
The Piedmont Inn - Hazelwood Exit, Waynesville.
Granny's Kitchen - US 19, Lake Junaluska
The Inn On Prospect Hill - 320 S. Main Street, Waynesville.
The Lodge - 118 Ninevah, Waynesville
Waynesville Country Club Inn
Bogart's Restaurant & Tavern - S. Main Street, Waynesville.
Alfredo's - Maggie Valley

* adv.

ACCOMMODATIONS:

TWINBROOK RESORT. *Rt. 1, Box 683, Maggie Valley, N. C. 28751.* Cottages set in secluded area and surrounded by forested peaks that rise to 6,000 feet. Three and four bedroom cottages completely furnished. All have fireplaces and electric heat. An ideal place to settle in while you explore and enjoy the Great Smoky Mountain area. Phone: 704/926-1388. *

Courtesy - Cataloochee Ranch

CATALOOCHEE RANCH
SKI AREA and SUMMER RESORT

CATALOOCHEE RANCH- "Mile High", *above Maggie Valley. US 19. (704) 926-1401, summer. (704) 926-0285 winter. Open all year.* Superb lodging, dining and recreation since 1939. Bordering the Great Smoky Mountains National Park, with 1,000 acres at 5,000 ft. elevation. Accommodations for about 40 guests in ranch house, converted barn and cabins. Riding, back-country trips, fishing, swimming, tennis. Skiing, mid-December-mid-March. Write for winter season brochure. **Mile High dining** - Ranch style lunch and dinner. Dining room open to public. Reservations by noon. (704) 926-1401. *Located 3 miles from Maggie, 13 miles from Waynesville, 40 miles from Asheville, Maggie Exit from I-40.* *

SHOP

IRWIN ANTIQUES - *US 19, Maggie Valley (704) 926-1525.* "This is a real antique shop". Country and Victorian antique furniture and old pattern glass. Formerly Foans Antiques. The new owners will carry on the tradition of quality. *

CHEROKEE INDIAN RESERVATION
Junction U.S. 19-441

The town of Cherokee is one of North Carolina's popular tourist attractions with many small shops, exhibits and amusements. The Cherokees are noted for their basketry, wood carving, pottery and bead work. You will have a wide selection. "Shop-hopping" is fun, but we urge you to go beyond the town for some of the other interesting and educational features near by. The last portion of the Blue Ridge Parkway goes through the Reservation before it terminates at US 441 on the Parkway at Milepost 469. The Blue Ridge Parkway was built to link the Shenandoah National Park in Virginia with the Great Smoky Mountains National Park.

HISTORY: The Cherokee Nation lived and worked as farmers in the Southern Appalachians. A high level of culture and civilization was reached under the guidance of such leaders as Sequoyah. National pride was strong, and an alphabet was invented by Sequoyah, thus enabling his people to be among the first literate Indians. During the Revolutionary War the Cherokees defended their land vigorously against the colonists and were allied with the British. Around 1820 they adopted a form of government modeled on that of the United States. The discovery of gold on their land precipitated a struggle with the U.S. government over the sale of their territory. In a reversal of an 1832 U.S. Supreme Court decision that the Cherokee Nation was an autonomus territory. Congress passed a bitterly contested Indian Removal Bill, and Georgia siezed the land. The Cherokees moved into Tennessee and built their last capitol near Chattanooga. The Indians were forced to cede much land, and in 1838, 7000 federal troops with volunteers and militia again forced an Indian relocation. Many were marched under guard as prisoners and taken to Oklahoma Territory. Four thousand died on the long tortuous journey. This "Trail of Tears" march, as it came to be known, was commemorated in April, 1978 at the Red Clay Council Grounds at Oldfort, Tenn. It will now be recognized as Red Clay State Park.

OCONALUFTEE VISITORS CENTER AND PIONEER FARMSTEAD.
Pioneer artifacts covering early life in the Southern Appalachians.

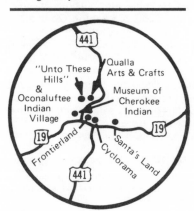

Museum of the Cherokee Indian, Cherokee, N. C.

Museum of the Cherokee Indian. A tragic history is relived in this magnificent museum. The center is considered the cultural heart of the Eastern Band of the Cherokee, and the visitor becomes involved with history through experiencing a variety of audio-visual aids. Charming legends are intermingled with historical facts; pictures and tape trace movements of early man to North America. Nature's gifts, and the ability to use them, formed the basis for a civilization that included an alphabet. Prehistoric artifacts and specimens display weaving, basketwork, pottery, and other arts and crafts of the Cherokees. Clovis and Cumberland projectile points date back more than 10,000 years. Grooved stone axes date between 5000 and 1000 B.C. Marine shell gorgets and carved dance masks are in the collection. There is much to see and much to learn, so do not rush your visit to this important museum.

Oconaluftee Indian Village. Oconaluftee Indian Village depicting a living Indian community of over 250 years ago opens to the public in mid-May and welcomes visitors on a daily basis until late October. Cherokee Indians demonstrate the way of life of ancient ancestors. Open daily mid-May thru late October.

73

|UNTO THESE HILLS DRAMA)

The outdoor drama **Unto These Hills** opens in mid-June and is presented through late August. Every night except Sunday finds hundreds of theatre goers enjoying this experience in a beautiful setting at the Mountainside theatre. As dusk fades, darkness replaces curtains and clever lighting draws the eye to set changes. Dr. Jack Kilpatrick, a Cherokee, wrote the music for **Unto These Hills.** Interpreted on a magnificent organ, the music - soft - light - thunderous -enhances the story written by Dr. Kermit Hunter. Dr. Hunter has written more than thirty historical dramas for outdoor productions throughout the United States. He is well known as a poet, teacher and musician. Many native Cherokees are in the large cast; other professional actors and dancers round out the troup of this magnificent performance. For additional information write: *Cherokee Historical Asso., P.O. Box 398, Cherokee, N.C. 28719. Phone: (704) 497-2111 for reservations. (Held till 8 p.m.)*

CHEROKEE, N.C.

Entertainment Schedule Mid-June to Mid-August
Saturday and Sunday Labor Day Weekend

FORT CHEROKEE - GUN FIGHT
SALOON SHOW - LAST CHANCE SALOON
LOG ROLLING SHOW - LAKE FRONT
INDIAN DANCE - INDIAN TERRITORY
EDDIE NASH SHOW - WHITE HORSE CAFE

GIFT SHOPS
RIDES FOR ALL AGES
WHIP AND
    ROPE EXHIBITIONS
GAME ROOM

Each show presented several times daily.

SANTA'S LAND PARK AND ZOO. *Hwy. 19 near Cherokee.* Daily May thru October. This clean well-run place is a real fantasy land. Parents and grandparents will enjoy it just as much as the youngsters. There is a scenic train ride around the park. Petting zoo, exotic birds, rare animals as well as deer and barnyard animals intrigue the children. One price admission includes it all and allows you to take the rides as many times as you wish. Santa and Mrs. Claus will give you a real welcome.

BOUNDARY TREE LODGE AND DINING ROOM. *U.S. 441.Open all year.* Restaurant and snack bar owned and operated by the Eastern Band of the Cherokees. The food is delicious and served in bright surroundings. North of Cherokee — last place before the Great Smoky Mountains National Park.

QUALLA ARTS AND CRAFTS MUTUAL, INC. *U.S. 441. (704) 497-3103. All year. Daily. Closed Sunday during winter.* An Indian cooperative craft shop. Qualla sells authentic work of the Cherokee and is a member of the southern Highland Handicraft Guild. Baskets, wood-carving, pottery and some work from New Mexico and Arizona Indians.

HEAVENLY FUDGE SHOPPE *Saunooke Shops, U.S. 441.* Look for the dove imprint on the boxes and bags of delicious fudge. Twelve different kinds and all super. This candy business has been an interesting adventure for the owners, and their customers are the lucky recipients of their skill. Milk chocolate lollipops for the kids. Your nose will lead you to the candy.

HENDERSON COUNTY
Established 1838

COUNTY SEAT: Hendersonville. *Elevation 2,146 Ft.*
COUNTY POPULATION: *58,580*
COMMUNITIES: *Hendersonville, Laurel Park, Flat Rock, Fletcher, Edneyville, Etowah, Horseshoe.*

Henderson County is famous for its apple industry. With over seven million bushels of apples annually, it is the largest producer in the state and ranks seventh in apple production in the nation. Henderson's moderate climate, beautiful mountain scenery, recreational and cultural activities make it an ideal summer resort, retirement community, and a popular center for summer camps. The county is interlaced with fine highways US 25, US 64 and Interstate 26. Write for detailed information: *Greater Hendersonville Chamber of Commerce, P.O. Box 489, Hendersonville, N.C. 28793. (704) 692-1413.*

EARLY HISTORY: Young war veteran William Mills was the first settler in what is now Henderson County. He was given one of the first land grants west of the Blue Ridge after the Revolutionary War in 1787. Mills settled in Fruitland and is remembered when apple blossoms cover the hills of Henderson County or when a fisherman hooks a big trout in Mills River. William Mills and his wife Eleanor started the Henderson County apple industry. Planting hundreds of apple trees each year, they were imitated by their neighbors until today Henderson County has 13,000 acres of commercial orchards. During the late 1700's, Samuel Edney also made his home in what is now Henderson County and became the first resident Methodist minister southwest of the Blue Ridge. The geography of the county was an asset to its growth. It was the broadest, most open valley to be found in all Western North Carolina and offered the easiest passageway from the South Carolina lowlands into the mountains. The area profited greatly after 1826-27 by the Buncombe Turnpike which ran the length of the County. By the early 1800's summer visitors began to build homes and make the annual pilgrimage to the mountains, prompting local historian Sadie Smathers Patton to name Flat Rock "the Little Charleston of the Mountains." The County of Henderson was established in 1838, and both county and county seat were named in honor of Judge Leonard Henderson of the state's Supreme Court. The original land for the county seat was given by Judge Mitchell King.

PICNICKING:

NORTH MILLS RIVER RECREATION AREA, *Pisgah National Forest. N. C. 191 south of Asheville.* *Turn on Forest Service Road 478.* Developed campground.

HOLMES STATE FOREST. *692-0100.* One of North Carolina's small State Forests. 231 Mountain acres in Henderson County. Forestry center, picnic pavilion and picnic area (25 tables), waterfalls, nature trails, game areas. Located on Crab Creek Rd. #1127 off the Kanuga Road, 10 miles from Hendersonville. Movie and "talking trees!"

Courtesy - N.C. Apple Festival

THE NORTH CAROLINA APPLE FESTIVAL
(Late August through Labor Day)

Henderson County is both bountiful and beautiful and is celebrated each year with an Apple Festival. Marking the culmination of summer's activities and the early harvest of Henderson County apples...weeks ahead of other apple producing states...the festival is a community party. The program of the festival has varied slightly from year to year but has always contained such well known features as the selection and crowning of a queen at the Beauty Pageant - second only to the Miss North Carolina Pageant. A gala coronation ball, tours of orchards, square dance and folk music events, special promotions by local merchants, the King Apple Parade (always on Labor Day), and the last street dance of the summer season (set for the early evening following the parade) complete the extensive plan for this major event.

HENDERSON COUNTY CURB MARKET. *221 South Church Street. (704) 692-8012.* A fifty year old tradition in Hendersonville, tourists moving through rows of booths will find home-churned butter, buttermilk, country lard, fruits, berries, cut flowers, potted plants, mountain herbs, rugs, quilts, aprons, sunbonnets, birdhouses, pies, cakes, bread, cookies, jams and jellies. Among the wares, city folks will find old fashioned goodies they haven't glimpsed in years. Sun-dried apples - cottage cheese - brown eggs and gourds. *Tues. Thurs, Sat, a.m.*

OPPORTUNITY HOUSE. *819 Fleming St. 692-0575. Open Mon.-Fri. Closed mid-December through January.* Twenty years as an arts, crafts and culture center where learning, serving and fellowship are the main objectives. Book and Gift Shop. Monthly Art exhibits.

SPECIALTY SHOPPING *

CAROLYN'S BOOK STORE. 599 N.Main St. (704) 693-5096. Excellent selection of N.C. Books.

BRASS LATCH AND RIGGS STAINED GLASS. 117 S. Main Street, Hendersonville, (704) 693-7505. A unique blending of country antiques, collectibles and stained glass and supplies. Also antique light fixtures, vintage clothing, gallery crafts, lamps, quilts and baskets.

THE LITTLE RED RIDING HOOD. 605 Kanuga St., Hendersonville. (704) 693-6427. Distinctive children's apparel sizes 0-7. Quality lines such as Florence Eiseman, Sylvia Whyte, Lil Filly, Feltman Brothers, Ruth Scharf. Infant accessories, imported toys, handmade dolls. A delightful shopping experience. Right off S. Main Street, .3 miles (3/10) on Kanuga St.

CLASSICS AND COLLECTABLE. 116-B North Main Street, Hendersonville. (704) 697-6586. Mon.-Sat. Attractive new shop in town. Variety of collectables. Baskets, glass, trunks, quilts. Unique small antique furniture especially suited for small homes. Primitive and Victorian pieces in excellent condition.

MINA MOESSEN HAND CRAFTS. 2846 Haywood Rd. Hwy. 191 N. (704) 692-4951. Closed Sunday. Generally considered the "best craft shop around," this shop continues a fine tradition of authentic crafts of this area. Quite a varied selection. Also four rooms of antiques and collectibles including furniture.

HERITAGE SQUARE MALL
121 Barnwell at Church St., Hendersonville, N.C.
Open all year. Closed Sunday.

Attractive shopping mall under one roof. The adaptive restoration of an old warehouse has created one of Hendersonville's most interesting shopping spots.

THE CENTURY SHOP. (704) 692-4160. A shop to please any antique lover. Great variety of brass, silver and old glass. Paintings, china, rugs, furniture, quilts and estate pieces. Many small gifts. Large range of prices. Auctions.

THE CRAFT SHOP. (704) 692-3341. Unique crafts and gifts made by local crafts people. Over 75 handmade Christmas tree ornaments. Also a nice selection of greeting cards and candles. Wood, ceramics, quilts and knits. Ship anywhere in U.S.

TRUDI'S CHEESE AND WINE SHOP. (704) 693-0811. Finest selection of domestic and imported wines and champagnes. Over 70 cheeses and more than 100 wines from around the world. Gourmet items, teas, spices and freshly ground coffees. Picnic baskets filled to order.

THE SAMOVAR CAFE. (704) 692-5981. Where dining is not only pleasing but also a relaxing break at midday. Specializing in homemade soups, desserts, quiches and delicious crepes, salads, sandwiches. Salad plates and meat platters.

HENDERSONVILLE TRAVEL,INC. (704) 693-0701. "Travel confidently" with this agency to care for all your travel needs. Member of ASTA. Airline tickets. Tours. Ships. Cruises. Independent travel. Hotel and car reservations. Mon.-Fri.: 9:00-5:30. Saturday: 10:00-2:00.

INNS AND RESTAURANTS

ECHO MOUNTAIN INN, *2849 Laurel Park Hwy. (2 mi. out 5th Ave., W.) Phone (704) 693-9626. Open all year.* This lovely mountain top Inn has an 85 year old history. You are welcomed by country charm and southern hospitality at a refreshing 3,000 foot elevation. Most rooms and apts. have a panoramic view of the Blue Ridge Mountains and the city below. All units are attractively furnished including Serta perfect sleeper beds and private baths. Three wholesome meals a day are served in the delightful dining room, also overlooking the mountains. Open to the public. Reservations requested. Sit on the porch, rock and enjoy the view. Beautiful swimming pool and shuffleboard courts. Also pool and ping pong. Small meeting room. *

Restaurants

FO-FO-TH-BO, LTD. *330 N. Main Street, Hendersonville. (704) 692-0429. Tues.-Sat.: 11 am - 9 pm. Sunday Brunch: 10 am - 3 pm. Closed Jan. and Feb.* Transcending the usual image of "natural foods" restaurants, Fo-Fo offers a tasteful variety of skillfully prepared, meatless foods, based on the cuisines of Southern Europe and the Middle East. A menu of fascinating variety is offered at lunch and dinner in an atmosphere that is elegant but comfortable. An ever-popular meal at Fo-Fo is the Sunday brunch. All brunches include blueberry muffins and a hot fruit appetizer. Dessert at Fo-Fo is spectacular; the specialty of the house is chocolate cheesecake. Domestic and imported wines are available and, in summer, fresh fruit sangria. *

Herb Garden - Main St.
Clifton's Cafeteria - 7th Ave. & Church
Home Food Shop Cafeteria - Main St.
Dutch Inn - US 25 - NC 191
The Village Inn - US 25 - Flat Rock.
Coach Lite - Skyland - exit I-26.
4th Ave. East Cabaret

THE DOWNTOWN SHOPPING PARK is a six block revitalization program which has created a park-like atmosphere including planting islands, sidewalk benches, angle parking and a gazebo for speech making and music.

* adv.

St. John in the Wilderness   Courtesy - Flat Rock Historical Society

FLAT ROCK
South of Asheville - U.S. 25 - I-26
Flat Rock Historic District entered in National Register of Historic Places

HISTORIC SKETCH. Flat Rock was aptly named "The Little Charleston of the Mountains" by historian Mrs. Sadie Smathers Patton. Mr. and Mrs. Charles Baring built the first of the great houses which were designed to take full advantage of cool mountain air and beautiful views. A family chapel was also built by the Barings (1833-34). It is the oldest Episcopal Church in Western North Carolina, given to the Diocese of North Carolina in 1836 and enlarged in 1852. St. John in the Wilderness is nestled in ivy, boxwood and evergreens and appropriately accented with wrought iron and Charleston Battery Benches.

KANUGA CONFERENCES. *Kanuga Rd. Hendersonville exit of I-26. (704) 692-9136. Open all year.* This is the nation's largest Episcopal Conference and camping center. Located on 1200 woodland acres, the buildings overlook Kanuga Lake. Accommodations range from modern Kanuga Lake Inn to the old timey screened porch cottages by the lake. This is the place to relax with time for tennis, swimming, boating, hiking or just sitting. Quiet informality is soothing to the spirit; visitors go home feeling well fed and refreshed. This Episcopal center is open to the public with two outstanding guest periods: summer guest period—mid-July thru August and "See the Leaves" the latter part of October. Special programs available. Camp Kanuga is a coeducational summer camp for children 8 to 15. *Mailing address: Kanuga, P.O. Drawer 250, Hendersonville, N. C. 28739.*

BON CLARKEN CONFERENCE GROUNDS. *U.S. 25 S., 692-2223. April through October.* Associate Reform Presbyterian Assembly. Residential community and cottages. Conference and convention facilities. 13 acre lake. Children's camp—gift shop.

OAKDALE CEMETERY. The inspiration for Thomas Wolfe's "Look Homeward Angel," is located in the Oakdale Cemetery in Hendersonville, 6th Ave. W. The statue was fashioned by Thomas Wolfe's father.

Woodfield Inn
FLAT ROCK, NORTH CAROLINA 28731

Courtesy - Woodfield Inn
"Over a Century of Hospitality"

WOODFIELD INN. *U.S. 25, South. (704) 693-6016.* Open all year. Western North Carolina's oldest inn with continuous operation. Originally situated on approximately 400 acres of land in the middle of the Flat Rock settlement, Woodfield Inn was completed between 1850-1852. Designed to replace small inadequate turnpike taverns Woodfield became an elegant center for summer vacations. The Inn attracted an endless stream of visitors and established Flat Rock as a famous summer resort. Historic Woodfields is now undergoing restoration, and with new management continues an unbroken tradition of southern hospitality. Comfortable bedrooms are furnished with antiques. Guests are served a continental breakfast. The excellent dining room is open to the public for lunch and dinner, serving continental cusine with pastries prepared in the special hotel bakery. Call for reservations. A new hotel feature is THE WOODFIELD TAP ROOM. Special arrangements can be made for wedding receptions and private parties. *

HISTORIC FLAT ROCK TOUR OF HOMES. *First Friday in August*
Enjoy the special treat of summer discovery during the Annual Historic Flat Rock Tour of Homes. Several beautiful houses are open to the public, as well as historic St. John of the Wilderness and Woodfield Inn. *Write: Historic Flat Rock, Inc., P. O. Box 295, Flat Rock, N. C. 28731.*

* adv.

Courtesy - Carl Sandburg Home

CARL SANDBURG HOME. *Connemara. National Historic Site. Open all year. Little River Road, off US 25 south of Hendersonville at Flat Rock.* Connemara (1839) was built as a summer home by Christopher Gustavus Memminger of Charleston. A great southern leader, he served as Secretary of the Tresury of the Confederacy. Carl Sandburg (1878-1967) and his family acquired the home in 1945 and enjoyed it for twenty-two years as a working farm and retreat for intellectual pursuits. *Connemara* reflects the simple life style of Carl Sandburg, Pulitzer Prize Winner and biographer of Abraham Lincoln. Thousands of books, musical instruments, an old typewriter and the pleasure of nature exemplify the Sandburg philosophy of work and living as an on-going project. On site parking is one third mile from main house. Visitors may use a shuttle bus or walking trail to reach the Sandburg home. Allow at least two hours for a guided tour of house, "On your own" use of trails and visit to farm area and goat herd. Admission is free. *Open daily but closed Thanksgiving, Christmas and New Year's.* Special Summer Outdoor Program at *Connemara.* 2:30 Daily except Wednesday and Saturday. *"The World of Carl Sandburg,"* thirty minute dramatic presentation of poetry and songs by the Vagabond Workshop Theatre Company. Entertainment for the family. *11:00 am Monday and Thursday "Rootabaga Stories"* for six weeks beginning in July.

FLAT ROCK PLAYHOUSE. *693-0731.* An outstanding summer season by the State Theatre of North Carolina. Organized in 1937, the Vagabond Players have entertained over three million patrons. Plays each week from the end of June through August. Evening performances and matinees Wednesday and Saturday. Tickets available for single plays or by the season. Free parking - picnic area. *The Playhouse was established on the grounds of the Flat Rock, a natural landmark for Indians and early pioneers.*

Courtesy - Forge Valley Fun Park

FORGE VALLEY FUN PARK. *Hwy. 280. S. Mills River between Henderson-* *sonville and Brevard. (704) 891-3134 or 891-3241.* Look for the Old Mill with its 16-foot water driven wheel in full operation. You will be headed in the right direction for an hour or a day of pleasure and excitement. Fun for the family and a new attraction in WNC.

PET ANIMAL PARK. The natural attraction! A collection of full size and miniature, exotic and domestic animals to be enjoyed. Feed, pet or watch baby animals - goats - calves - lambs. Learn about emus, rheas, llamas, kangaroos, and zebu cattle. Get to know the Capuchin moneys, Winkin, Blinkin and Nod, and Scotty the Scotish Highlander bull. Take in the daily puppet show or weekend Blue Grass Band.

PLAYGROUND. Have you ever dreamed of a giant tree house? Forge Valley has one with spiral slides, climbing ladders and a swinging bridge. Family picnic tables nearby.

In the Grist Mill Complex:

POTTERY SHOP: Potter at work. Pottery for sale and custom orders.

GENERAL STORE. Everything from "eggs to overalls". And breads and cake from THE STONE OVEN BAKERY, on the premises.

MOUNTAIN CRAFT SHOP. Impressive collection of local crafts.

ICE CREAM SHOP. A sweet stop for lunch or ice cream. Sandwiches and fountain goodies. **Park open daily 10 a.m. - *6 p.m. May through October.* Full service restaurant planned for 1982. ***

Jackson County Courthouse, Sylva, North Carolina   *N.C. Travel and Tourism Division*
Photo - Clay Nolen.

JACKSON COUNTY
INCORPORATED TOWNS: *Sylva, Dillsboro, Webster*
OTHER TOWNS: Cullowhee, Cashiers, Balsam, Whittier.
COUNTY SEAT: *Sylva. Elevation 2,047 Ft.*
POPULATION OF JACKSON COUNTY: *25,811*

Jackson County has a high elevation with peaks towering above stream-fed valleys. It is enclosed by five major mountain ranges. The annual maximum temperature (July and August) is 86 degrees. Average annual is 58 degrees. Forest products and water power are abundant in Jackson County. Olivine is mined and processed locally for steel manufacturing. Scenic beauty reigns in every part of the county. Cashiers Valley, Sapphire Valley, Whiteside Mt. (elev. 4,930) and Bridal Veil Falls are a few of the inviting areas.

HISTORY: Named for Andrew Jackson, President of the United States, born in Mecklenburg County, North Carolina.

In 1851, Jackson County was formed from sections of Haywood and Macon counties and named for Andrew Jackson. It embraced a rugged mountain area that for an uncharted time had been a part of the Cherokee homeland. The native Americans had left one of the few hieroglyphic inscriptions to be found in Western North Carolina - the Judaculla Rock. Strange markings have been uncipherable to Cherokees and white men, however some students of history think it is a Cherokee diagram of a battle. Jackson County was the scene of bloodshed during struggles between Cherokees and the whites.

Among the early settlers in the county was a group of French Hugenots from South Carolina who came to Tuckasegee Valley and named their settlement East La Porte.

JACKSON COUNTY CHAMBER OF COMMERCE, *18 N. Central St., Sylva, NC 28779 - (704) 586-2155*

Western Carolina University - Cullowhee, N.C.   *Photo - Harry Duke*

WESTERN NORTH CAROLINA UNIVERSITY: Founded in 1889, it now enrolls 6700 students. One of sixteen campuses of the University of North Carolina, the 400 acre campus is located in Cullowhee, North Carolina. Situated in a valley, it is surrounded by some of the highest mountains in Eastern North America. The university has six schools: Art and Sciences, Business, Technology and Applied Science, Nursing and Health Service, Education and Psychology, and the Graduate School. There is a full scale ROTC program on campus. The university awards a number of academic and endowed scholarships as well as other grants. There are nine resident halls located near dining and classroom facilities. For additional information write: *The Admissions Office, 220 University Administration/Mountain Heritage Center, Cullowhee, N.C. 28723. Ph: (704) 227-7317.*

MOUNTAIN HERITAGE CENTER. Western Carolina University, Cullowhee, N. C. (704) 227-7129. Museum with changing exhibitions focusing on natural, Indian and pioneer heritage audio-visual mulit-image presentation. Open Mon. - Fri. 9 a.m. - 4 p.m. and Sunday afternoon during summer.

DILLSBORO

U.S. 23-19A—441 West of Asheville

The Dillsboro run is a favorite trek for craft enthusiasts. Forty-nine scenic miles from Asheville.

The Jarrett House   Photo - The Herald Publishing Co.

COUNTRY INN

JARRETT HOUSE. *US 441 S., Dillsboro. (704)586-9964. Exit 441 from 19A-23 Bypass.* One of the oldest inns in Western North Carolina, the Jarrett House was built in 1884 during the era of the horse and buggy and the wood-burning passenger train. William Allen Dills built the Inn after the Western North Carolina Railway opened the area to "comers and stayers." Comfort and good food were the attractions, and the Inn became the official dining place for passengers and employees of the railroad. The passenger train from Asheville stopped at noon for dinner, and the number of reservations was telegraphed ahead from Balsam. Purchased by Jim and Jean Hartbarger, the Inn retains its reputaion for good food, "just as it's been from the beginning." Bountiful daily menu includes country ham and red-eye gravy, fried chicken, mountain trout, fresh vegetables and honey with hot biscuits. Three meals a day. Twenty-two guest rooms with period furniture. An old-fashioned treat. *Write: P.O. Box 219, Dillsboro, N.C. 28725. Closed winter months.* *

86   * adv.

DILLSBORO

RIVERWOOD SHOPS.

NANCY TUT'S Christmas Shop. Open Late March-December. Ph: 586-5391. A small world full of the wonder of Christmas. Two floors of miniatures, dollhouses, imported decorations. Hummels, dolls and needlework.

RIVERWOOD PEWTER SHOP. Hand-hammered pewter: bowls, plates, platters, etc. See artisans at work. Tea and coffee services, mugs, goblets. Member Southern Highland Handicraft Guild.

THE CHEDDAR BOX. Ph: 586-4442. Imported cheeses, fancy foods, gourmet kitchen gadgets and gifts. Teas, custom ground coffees and delicious fudge.

RIVERWOOD HANDWEAVING. Handwoven articles, looms, weaving supplies, books and yarns. A delightful weaving studio.

THE WELL HOUSE. Hot deli sandwiches, salads, cheesecake served in a relaxed turn-of-the-century atmosphere.

RIVERWOOD CRAFT SHOP. Ph.: 586-2547. Open 9-5 Mon.-Sat. year round. Specializing in crafts of Southern Highlands. Gifts for everyone.

RIVERWOOD POTTERY. Unique stoneware and porcelain designs by David Lee.

RIVERWOOD MENAGERIE. Prints, drawings, blown glass, fine Tiffany-style leaded glass.

THE OLD SCHOOL. *Rt. 441 S. 4 miles from Dillsboro.* A shopping complex. **MJ'S TOLE HOUSE.** Art work on everything from bells to pots and crocks. **THE COUNTRY MOUSE.** Traditional quilts and afghans-antique toys. **TIMES PAST.** 10,000 antique items from 9 dealers. Crank phones, spinning wheels, etc. **T 'n B TREASURES.** Handmade items old and new, wood, raffia and straw. **THIS & THAT SHOP.** Hand fashioned lamps from unusual bases. Indian artifacts. **SANTA'S FAVORITES.** Family makes ornaments plus work from 15 other crafters. **HANDMADE JEWELRY.** Gemstones, ivory, ebony and other exotic woods in rings, pins, etc. **HOUSE OF THE PAST ANNEX.** Ancient postcards, magazines, music, records. **ENCHANTING TREASURES.** Handcrafted southwestern Indian Jewelry - turquoise in silver and gold. **LOG CABIN ANTIQUES.** Old beds, dressers, washstands and chairs. Also wicker and brass.

HICKORY SMOKEHOUSE RESTAURANT.* *Hwy. 441. Ph.: 586-6933. 5 miles south of Dillsboro, N.C. 11:30 a.m. to 8 p.m. Daily. Closed Wednesday.* Steaks, Bar-B-Que, Seafoods.

MOUNTAIN BROOK COTTAGES.* *Rt. 441 S. Sylva, N.C. P.O. Box 301. Ph.: (704)586-4329.* Stone and log cottages with fireplaces. Fully equipped kitchens and everything else provided for cottage comfort. Porch swings, babbling brooks and waterfalls nearby to delight you. Grocery items, launderette and restaurant close by. Rentals on weekly basis. For detailed information and reservations write address above.

* adv.

CASHIERS—SAPPHIRE

High Hampton Inn

HIGH HAMPTON INN. *Cashiers, N.C.* Sitting handsomely on a Lake beneath a stone-faced mountain, this famous old inn is located on historic property that was once the home of General Wade Hampton. A loyal following of visitors come year after year for the natural beauty, the mild climate, and the atmosphere of relaxed summer living. Rooms at the inn or spacious cottages with sitting rooms and fireplaces are available. Numerous activities all summer include special golf and tennis packages, a school of equitation for girls, ages 10 to 16, lawn bowling, shuffleboard, boating, fishing and swimming. There is an 18 hole golf course with two practice greens and a practice driving range. Tennis buffs will find fast-dry courts and a practice area. Thanksgiving brings an annual houseparty that begins with cocktails on Wednesday evening and extends through Sunday. A children's program for this event includes picnics and hayrides. Several privately owned cottages near High Hampton are sometimes available on a rental basis. Weekly (Sunday to Sunday) on American or European plan. Write: *High Hampton Inn, Cashiers, North Carolina, 28717.* Ph: *704/743-2411.* *

Photo - Fairfield Communities, Inc.

FAIRFIELD INN

FAIRFIELD SAPPHIRE VALLEY-FAIRFIELD INN. *US 64, three miles east of Cashiers. Ph.: (704)743-3441.* Built in 1896 as a country retreat for the wealthy, this prestigious old inn has been a landmark since the turn of the century. Overlooking Lake Fairfield, it faces Bald Rock, an imposing mountain of sheer granite; there is no finer view. Guests may sit on the terrace or in the patio room to enjoy the beauty and peacefulness broken only by crickets and bobwhites calling. The Mountain Porch and Country club feature traditional mountain dishes and gourmet dining. Fairfield Sapphire Valley has two beautiful championship golf courses. Eighteen holes of George Cobb design set in a rolling, peaceful valley and eighteen holes of challenging mountain terrain to be completed in spring 1982. Carefully manicured bent grass greens and bridges of native stone over rushing streams make the game memorable. Cottages and luxurious villas are available for rent on a daily, weekly, or monthly basis. Conference participants will find the latest in facilities and equipment in this gentle mountain setting. The newest John Newcombe Tennis Center has eight har-tru and two hard surface courts. Fishing, boating, horseback riding, and hiking are offered - plus an exciting program of activities planned by an innovative Recreation Department. A gem mine once worked by Tiffany's available to guests. From hayrides to snow skiing - we've got it all. Truly a four season resort. *Write: Fairfield Sapphire Valley, Star Route 70, Box 80, Sapphire, N.C. 28774.* *

* adv.

CASHIERS

LYN K. HOLLOWAY ANTIQUES. *At the crossroads in Cashiers. Summer.* Long established as one of the finest antique shops in the western part of North Carolina. A cottage and annex filled to overflowing with beautiful furniture and accessories. Distinctive choices artfully arranged in every room. English, American and Oriental. *

RESTAURANTS

YESTERDAY'S LTD. An old house charmingly revamped to create a first rate restaurant. All fresh foods perfectly prepared and perfectly delicious. Space shared with a flower shop in a glass enclosed room. Open all year for luncheon, dinner and Sunday brunch. *July through Mid-August, 7 days. Reservations requested. Brown bag permit. Ph.: (704) 743-3101. Hwy. 107.* *

CORNUCOPIA. *Hwy. 107 South.* This Victorian style restaurant occupies the building that once housed the Cashiers Post Office. There is a spacious open deck to enjoy lunch and dinner. Marvelous selection of delectables plus offerings from the new rotisserie. *(Ph: 743-3750.* *

THE RED DOOR. *U.S. 64. Near Sapphire and Cashiers.* Gourmet dining. Dinner by candle light. True gourmet selections including chicken cordon bleu, beef tenderloin, veal scallopini, shrimp scampi and frog legs. Open Wed.-Sun., June-October. Weekends remainder of the year. Brown bagging. Reservations please. *

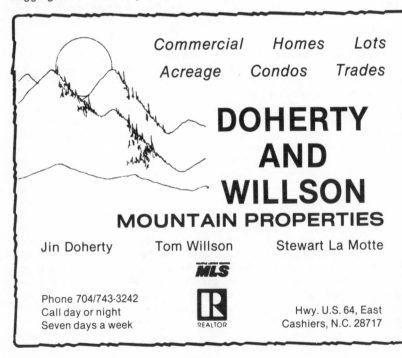

Commercial Homes Lots

Acreage Condos Trades

DOHERTY AND WILLSON

MOUNTAIN PROPERTIES

Jin Doherty   Tom Willson   Stewart La Motte

MLS

Phone 704/743-3242
Call day or night
Seven days a week

Ⓡ REALTOR

Hwy. U.S. 64, East
Cashiers, N.C. 28717

*adv.

MACON COUNTY
Established 1828

COUNTY SEAT: *Franklin. Elevation: 2,113 Ft.*
COUNTY POPULATION: *20,178.*
PRINCIPAL TOWNS: *Franklin and Highlands.*

CHAMBER OF COMMERCE INC., 180 Porter Street, Franklin, N. C. 28734 - 704/524-3161.

In Macon County the Cullasaja Gorge connects Franklin and Highlands the highest incorporated town in eastern United States.

HISTORY: During the years 1817-1819 the U.S. Government and the State of North Carolina, by treaties with the Cherokee Indians, acquired lands east of the Nantahala Mountains, and white settlers began to move into the area. In 1828 the North Carolina General Assembly passed legislation creating Macon County, and in the same year the first house was built. After the Civil War the community prospered, and by 1908 the Tallulah Falls Railroad had been built and there were many churches, schools, business establishments and a library. Macon County was the first county in the state to have compulsory school attendance. Today, several old buildings have been restored, and one building (1895) is now an art gallery. The county is famous for its gem mining and is a mecca for rock collectors. Several of the ruby and sapphire mines are located in nearby Cowee Valley. Most are open to the public and charge a modest fee for gem mining. Shops offering rough stones and finished jewelry are located in Franklin and Cowee Valley.

FRANKLIN

FRANKLIN GEM AND MINERAL MUSEUM
Housed in 150 year old Macon County Jail. Gem and Mineral specimens displayed by state and county locations. Gems, fossils, minerals, flourescents. Gift shops.

Following is a partial listing of the mines. There are so many, and you will want to choose your own stop. All are on Route 4 out of Franklin. Some have better facilities than others, as you will discover. Most offer digging on your own, or you may buy by the bucket. Usually entry fee. All have flumes for washing. **JONES — JACOBS — GREGORY'S — SCHULER — GIBSON — HOLBROOK** are just a few that we recommend.

Shops
Cowee Valley Lapidary. Rt. 4 at Ruby Mines. Franklin.

Dr. Sherman's Gem Shop - Clarks Chapel. Franklin.

Ruby City Gems - Franklin.

Zebo's Gem Shop - US 441 (business) Franklin.

Maco Crafts (see ad this section).

Christian Handcrafts - near Otto.

Bachelor's End Antiques - US 28 North Franklin.

Wiebe's Emporium Antiques - US 64 East. Franklin.

High Country Bookstore - Heritage Hollow.

Gem-Boree sponsored by Chamber late July- early Aug. Lectures, slides, exhibits, dealers. Modest admission. Macon County Community Bldg. US 441 South.

MACON COUNTY: *Nantahala National Forest Recreation Areas:*

WAYAH BALD. *US 64 southwest of Franklin; right on NC 1310; right on Forest Service Rd. 69.* Stone observation tower permits views of the Blue Ridge, Smoky, Cowee, Unicoi, Fish Hawk, Snowbird, Balsam, and Nantalhala Mountains. Laurel, azalea, and rhododendron abound. Picnicking at Wayah Crest.

STANDING INDIAN CAMPGROUND. *US 64 west of Franklin; turn left on Forest Service Rd. 67.* Developed campground along Nantahala River.

DRY FALLS. *US 64 northwest of Highlands. Visitors can walk behind Cullasaja River waterfall. Parking area. No picnicking or camping facilities.*

CLIFFSIDE LAKE. *US 64 northwest of Highlands; turn right on Forest Service Road 57.* Developed campground. Swimming, hiking, fishing.

VAN HOOK GLADE. *US 64 northwest of Highlands.* Scenic waterfalls. Developed campground. Picnic area. High elevation.

GLEN FALLS SCENIC AREA. *NC 106 southwest of Highlands.* River drops 50 feet over sharp ledge. Trail leads to falls. Parking available. No camping or picnicking facilities.

Shops

THE PANTRY KEY. *48 Highlands Road, Franklin, N.C. Ph.: (704) 369-9826.* A gift and gourmet shop specializing in cooking and serving accessories. Gourmet foods, spices, catering, home baked goods. Fun to visit, browse, and watch the working kitchen. *Located East Franklin Shopping Center.* Owned and operated by Adelaide D. Key. *

MACO CRAFTS INC. *Hwy. 441 South, Franklin. Ph.: 524-7878.* Mountain crafts from Western North Carolina residents. Fine quality and great variety. Quilts, custom made furniture, pottery, stained glass, toys and many, many other items. Now the home of the world's largest quilt which was on display at the Kennedy Center in Washington, D.C. in 1980. MACO sponsors annual "Spring Fling" craft celebration. *

Accommodations and Restaurants

Lullwater Inn - US 64 Franklin. 704/524-6532
Poor Richard's Inn (see ad this section).
Panther Bill's Storehouse Restaurant - Heritage Hollow.
McClure Farm Restaurant - US 441 South. Franklin.
Franklin Terrace Ice Cream Parlour. - 67 Harrison. Franklin.

Courtesy -
Asheville Chamber of Commerce

Gem Mining in Cowee Valley

World's Largest Quilt

Maco Crafts

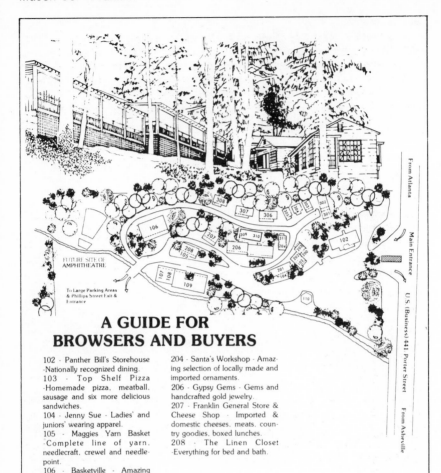

A GUIDE FOR
BROWSERS AND BUYERS

102 - Panther Bill's Storehouse -Nationally recognized dining.
103 - Top Shelf Pizza -Homemade pizza, meatball, sausage and six more delicious sandwiches.
104 - Jenny Sue - Ladies' and juniors' wearing apparel.
105 - Maggies Yarn Basket -Complete line of yarn, needlecraft, crewel and needlepoint.
106 - Basketville - Amazing selection of baskets, buckets & woodenware.
107 - Fudge N' Nut Shop - Fresh fudge brittles, candies, mountain taffy, salted-in-shell peanuts.
108 - Linda's Quilting Cabin - All your quilting needs. Custom made quilts, crafts & classes.
109 - The Way Station - Division of Tanner of N.C. Better women's apparel at discount prices.
110 - Gazebo
200 - Heritage Realty - Quality homes, land sales, contractors.
201 - Music Saloon - Tapes, records and accessories.
202 - High Country Book Store -Books of all kinds, puzzles, games.
203 - What Knots? - Complete line of macrame supplies, gifts, lessons.

204 - Santa's Workshop - Amazing selection of locally made and imported ornaments.
206 - Gypsy Gems - Gems and handcrafted gold jewelry.
207 - Franklin General Store & Cheese Shop - Imported & domestic cheeses, meats, country goodies, boxed lunches.
208 - The Linen Closet -Everything for bed and bath.

CRAFTSMAN'S ROW

301 - Unicorn Glass Studio -Stained glass.
302 - Craft Shop
303 - Zsu Zsa - Art gallery
304 - Wood Butcher
305 - Heritage Hollow Office
306 - Cozy Cottage - Unique gifts and accessories.
307 - Craft Shop

308 - Brown Branch Pottery -Hand thrown pottery made on premises.
390 - Wax Menagerie - Hand carved candles made on premises.
310 - Craft Shop
311 - Primitives Unlimited - Handcrafted furniture and accessories.

A Distinctive Village of Shops
Franklin, North Carolina

HIGHLANDS

HISTORY: *Early in 1875, two young New Englanders, S.T. Kelsey and C.C. Hutchinson, purchased 800 acres of land on the crest of the Blue Ridge. The town of Highlands was established and the dream of a summer mountain resort took root. Progress was slow, but in the early 1900's, settlers arrived and gradually word spread about the magnificent climate and scenery. Hotels, stores, churches, a school and library were constructed and a newspaper began publication. The new town was established. Today the two original houses still stand on Main Street. The first hotel, the Highlands Inn, continues as a well loved landmark. Summer populations swells to around 12,000. Many beautiful houses dot the ridges, coves and slopes.*

Dry Waterfalls   **Courtesy - Asheville Chamber of Commerce**

RESTAURANTS *

Frog and Owl Cafe. Buck Creek Rd. Highlands, N. C. Ph: 526-5500. Reservations required. Open lunch and dinner Tues.-Sat., Sunday Buffet. Excellent food served beautifully in rustic surroundings. This mountainside restaurant has a loyal following of guests who appreciate every unique detail. Charming and distinctive.

Hildegard's. Main St. Ph: 526-3807. Gourmet food in a unique and charming setting. Member Greater Atlanta Chef's Association, Chaine Des Rotisseurs. Bavarian ambience in a lovely old house set back a bit from the street. Delightful menus. Serving 6 to 9:30 P.M.

Highlander Restaurant. Main St. Ph: 526-3169. Real down-home cooking. Homemade pies and breads. Luncheon served 11 to 3. Dinner 5 to 9 except Sundays.

Big John's Sirloin Room. Behind the Highlander Restaurant. Ph: 526-3169. Serving prime steaks, seafoods and lamb chops. Summer hours 6 to 9:30. Closed Sundays.

SHOPS *

The Royal Scot. Main St. Ph: 526-5917. Antiques and art gallery. American and English antiques - brass accessories. Gallery features contemporary artists. Open May - Oct. 10:00 to 5:00. A fine place to find the basics for your summer home.

The Stone Lantern. Main St. Ph: 526-2769. Art treasures from the Orient. 17th-19th century porcelains, bronzes, ivory, cloisonne and jade.

Cyrano's Bookshop. Main St. Ph: 526-5488. This shop is intentionally small, but it has access to 600,000 books in print. Finding out-of-print titles is Cyrano's speciality. Open all year.

Burlap Bag Shop. Martha's Lane at U.S. 64. Ph: 526-3033. May and June through Oct. **Burlap Bag Crafts. Teak Jungle - Artist's Corner - Crabtree and Evelyn - Village Lapidary - Beauty Salon - Timothy Restaurant.**

Highland's Village Square. Next to Postoffice. **Butterchurn Antiques - Sunbonnet Designs - Jeans South - Betty's of Jamaica - Enchanted Needle.**

HAPPENINGS IN HIGHLANDS

Highland's Playhouse. A professional summer stock company presents plays and musicals from June until Labor Day. Ph: 526-2695. Call for reservations and times of performance.

Helen's Barn. Dancing gets going on Friday and Saturday nights. Over 50 years of fun and rolicking pleasure at Helen's. Ph: 526-3823. June-Labor Day.

WHITESIDE MOUNTAIN. *U.S. 64 between Highlands and Cashiers.* Now a part of Nantahala National Forest, Whiteside Mountain, with a 2000 foot face, is the highest sheer precipice in Eastern America.

MADISON COUNTY
Established 1851

COUNTY SEAT: Marshall. *Elevation 1,650 Ft.*
COUNTY POPULATION: *16,827*
COMMUNITIES: *Marshall, Mars Hill, Hot Springs, Wolfe Laurel.*
Named for President James Madison, the county was established in 1851. Madison County is well known for its college community and surrounding country fed by the mighty French Broad River. The Pisgah National Forest's 49,000 acres supply extensive outdoor recreation. Skiing, golf, and white water rafting are popular sports, and the Appalachian Trail goes through Hot Springs. The town of Marshall sits beside the French Broad with the county school on an island in the river. It is said that Marshall is "one street wide, one mile long and sky high."

EARLY HISTORY. A central factor in the history of Madison County is the French Broad River. Indian routes came through Paint Rock and followed the river to the present site of Hot Springs. Later the river brought settlers into this region. Using the old Indian trail into the heart of Madison County, speculators acquired land for timber and agriculture. In 1788 Indian scouts discovered Warm Springs near the river, which became a favorite stopping place for travelers. First a tavern then a hotel was constructed. By 1800 the Warm Springs Hotel was famous for its hospitality and the curative powers of the waters. It was Western North Carolina's first health resort. In 1882 the railroad was completed; the large new Mountain Park Hotel was built on the old site. In 1886 with one of the first golf courses in the southeast, Hot Springs was hailed as a most desirable resort. Fire destroyed most of the main buildings in the 1920's. The springs are now on private land.

MARS HILL COLLEGE

MARS HILL COLLEGE. *US 19-23. (704) 689-1217. Twenty miles north of Asheville.* Established in 1856 it is the oldest institution in WNC still operating on original site. Campus of 150 acres at an elevation of 2,330 feet assures delightful environment for summer attractions:
RURAL LIFE MUSEUM. Preserving lifestyle of average mountain family 100-150 years ago. Early settler's home, furniture, tools, artifacts. *Open Tues.-Fri. Special tours. 689-1244.*
THE APPALACHIAN ROOM. Photographic archives. Regional books. Bascom Lamar Lunsford Applachian Music Archives. Memorial Library. *689-1244*
THE COUNTRY BOUTIQUE. *On campus.* Craftshop managed by Madison County Crafts Association. Outstanding quality in quilts, toys, carvings, instruments. Shop is housed in Old Frog Level Schoolhouse, restored.
THE SOUTHERN APPALACHIAN REPERTORY THEATER. Western North Carolina's only professional repertory theater. Fine plays in Owen Theater *Tuesday through Sunday. Mid June through first week in August.* Box office: *(704) 689-1239.*
THE BASCOM LAMAR LUNSFORD MOUNTAIN MUSIC AND DANCE FESTIVAL. Features mountain musicians, dance teams, craftsmen. *On campus in October. (704) 689-1332.*

Madison Co.

"Deep Water Rapids"   **Photo - Nicholas Hancock**

SMOKY MOUNTAIN RIVER EXPEDITIONS. Box 398, Hot Springs, N. C. 28743 (704) 622-7260. April-October. Guided raft trips on the scenic and exciting French Broad River, all equipment and lunch provided. Trips run daily on the thrilling Ocoee and Nolichucky Rivers in Tenn. Whitewater canoe instruction, rental and sales. Group rates available. GO FOR IT! Directions: US 25-70, 1 hour from Asheville - 2 hours from Knoxville.*

WOLF LAUREL RESORT ·

WOLF LAUREL. *US 23. 27 miles north of Asheville. (704)689-4111.* A complete 5,000 acre mountain resort rising to elevations of over 5,500 feet. Golf, skiing, tennis, swimming, horseback riding, set among high peaks and the freshness of nature. Wolf Laurel is a "second home" development, attracting residents from all over the U.S. *

WOLF LAUREL INN. (78 rooms) and MOUNTAIN TOP RESTAURANT. Also log cabins, cottages, "A" frames, contemporary homes with cooking facilities, 2 day minimum, completely furnished. Write: *Wolf Laurel Reservations, Rt. 3, Mars Hill, N.C. 28754. (704) 689-4111.*

WOLF LAUREL GOLF COURSE. 18 hole golf course, thrilling and visually spectacluar. Number 12 is highest hole east of the Rockies. Golfers can see Big Bald Mountain the 5,516 ft. peak overlooking the resort.

MOUNTAIN LAUREL CAMPGROUND AND COUNTRY STORE. *Off US 23. 28 miles north of Asheville. (704) 689-3602.* Good location near North Carolina-Tennessee line. Family campground for RV's and tents. All facilities for comfort and convenience. Camp sites secluded, private and shaded by trees and mountain laurel. Trout fishing in stocked ponds and area streams. Enjoy "Old Swimming Hole," picnic shelter, and quarter horse ranch. **COUNTRY STORE.** Formerly a post office built of chestnut, the store is 100 years old. Supplies, groceries and convenience items for campers. Also exceptional crafts. Custom orders in one of a kind gifts. Homebaked bread. All to the tune of a player piano. *

ROCKY BLUFF RECREATION AREA. *N.C. 209 south of Hot Springs.* Camping, picnicking, hiking, fishing.

98   * adv.

McDOWELL COUNTY
Established 1842

COUNTY SEAT: Marion. *Elevation 1,437 Ft.*
COUNTY POPULATION: *35,135*
COMMUNITIES: *Marion, Little Switzerland, Old Fort*

McDowell County brings together two separate elements of North Carolina lifestyle. A border county, McDowell reflects the industrialization of the Piedmont and the traditional atmosphere of a rural area. McDowell is a gateway to the magnificent mountain region of Western North Carolina and eastern Tennessee. The southern and eastern parts of the county are low in elevation. Northern and western sections climb to an elevation above 5,000 feet. Major highways, north-south US 221 and east-west I-40 intersect the county. The Blue Ridge Parkway runs along its northern border. Furniture and textile manufacturing contribute to the economy. You will find extensive recreational opportunities, fishing and camping. *For more information: McDowell Chamber of Commerce, 20 N. Logan St., Marion, N.C. 28752. (704) 652-4240. Pisgah National Forest — Grandfather Ranger District: District Ranger, U.S. Forest Service, P.O. Box 519, Marion, N.C. 28753. (704) 652-2144. Library Bldg.*

EARLY HISTORY: McDowell County was formed in 1842 from portions of Rutherford and Burke Counties, and was named for Major Joseph McDowell of Pleasant Gardens. A hero in the Battle of King's Mountain, McDowell fought in this decisive battle of the American Revolution which symbolized the end of British rule in America. The land of McDowell County was settled early. By 1776 this colonial frontier was marked by a fort (Old Fort) which protected the border settlers from Catawba and Cherokee attacks.

OVERMOUNTAIN VICTORY TRAIL. *First week in October.* Volunteer marchers in buckskin garb commemorate defeat of British at King's Mountain, October 7, 1780. Trail winds through McDowell County to King's Mountain.

MOUNTAIN GATEWAY MUSEUM. *Water Street, Old Fort, 10 am-5 pm Mon.-Sat., Sun. afternoon.* The museum depicts pioneer life in Western North Carolina with a splendid collection of artifacts. The focal point of the museum is the stone fireplace. There are cooking utensils of great variety. The museum's collection includes North Carolina pottery, maps, musical instruments, home remedies, and authentic pioneer cabins furnished in mountain style. A project of the Old Fort Historic Site's Committee and the State Department of Archives & History.

LINVILLE GORGE WILDERNESS. *U.S. 221 north of Marion, N. C. 183 E. to N.C. 105.* 7,600-acre area of rugged terrain. Entrance permit required. Developed picnic area. Parking area at Wiseman's View. Permits and trail maps available at District Ranger's office, Marion, N. C.

LINVILLE CAVERNS. *US 221 north of Marion.* Limestone caverns cleared and lighted. Admission fee.

LAKE JAMES. *Northeast of Marion via NC 221 and NC 126.* One of the best developed mountain lakes. Ideal fishing and water sports. Highway circling lake with numerous boat landings. Cabins and boats for rent. Picnicking on shore and islands in lake. Campsites.

The Carson House
McDowell County~Marion, N.C.

CARSON HOUSE. *US 70 west of Marion. Pleasant Gardens. Open May 1 - Oct. 31. Daily 10 am - 5 pm. (704) 724-4263.* Entered in National Register of Historic Places. Carson House was built by Colonel John Carson about 1780, and was the center of much of the early history of McDowell County. A charming museum featuring period rooms.

ANDREWS GEYSER. *Located 2 miles off US 70 up Mills Creek Road. Exit Old Fort from I-40.* Residents of Old Fort restored the geyser. A spring shoots a stream of water 200 feet in the air. Picnic area.

OLD FORT PICNIC AREA. *Off Old US 70 west of Old Fort.* Very good picnic area of Pisgah National Forest.

CURTIS CREEK AUTO TOUR. *From Old US 70 east of Old Fort take Forest Service Road #482.* One hour trip into the natural beauty of the mountains, with 12 optional stops. Enjoy this wildlife sanctuary.

McDOWELL HOUSE. *Pleasant Gardens US 70 west of Marion.* Ancestral colonial home of Joseph McDowell. built in the late 1780's the house has undergone many changes in ownership, but still retains its historic charm. It is now a shop.

CROSSBOW INTERNATIONAL RESTAURANT. *Lady Marion Plaza, Marion, N.C.* 652-5766. Popular restaurant with international cuisine.

RAMBLE RACK, INC. *207 East Court St., (704) 652-4950.* **The** outlet in Marion. For the family.

THE SHOE HOUSE. *US 70 near Carson House. (704) 724-4303.*

CAROLINA MOUNTAIN CRAFTS. *(704) 652-9111 in Marion.*

BLUE RIDGE PARKWAY. Unique feature in north McDowell County where Blue Ridge, Craggy and Black Mountains merge. Easily accessible from Marion *via US 221, US 70 and NC 226, 226A, and NC 80.*

LITTLE SWITZERLAND. *US 226A. Just off Blue Ridge Parkway.* An old resort community on crest of the Blue Ridge with inn, motels, cottages, and shops. Gorgeous views from Alpine Lookout south on NC 226A. Mineral shop for rockhounds. Glen Laurel hiking and horseback trail. One mile hike to 30 foot Grassy Creek Fall.

MITCHELL COUNTY
Established 1861
COUNTY SEAT: BAKERSVILLE. *Elevation 2,550 Ft.*
COUNTY POPULATION: *14,428*
PRINCIPAL TOWNS: *Spruce Pine, Bakersville, Roan Mountain, Little Switzerland*

HISTORY: Named in honor of Dr. Elisha Mitchell, Professor University of North Carolina. A log courthouse for the county was built in 1867. Traveling was difficult over rough mountain roads, and the county remained isolated for many years. In 1903, after the coming of the railroad, Spruce Pine became an active center for trade, the shipment of produce, and recreation. Mitchell County embraces 220 square miles and 17,502 acres of Pisgah National Forest. Lumber, ornamental shrubs and farm produce are produced today, along with furniture and textile manufacturing, and the processing of native minerals. A mountainous county, Mitchell elevations range for 1700 to 6300 feet. Tourism contributes to the economy and Spruce Pine is just 6 miles from the Blue Ridge Parkway.

MINERAL AND GEM FESTIVAL: Held annually in early August, this festival brings the "rock hounds" from miles away. There are at least eleven mines in the Spruce Pine area. Most are within 13 miles of the town. A list of the minerals and gems found would include: Hyalite, Autunite, Garnet, Mica, Emerald, Tourmaline, Columbite, Forbenite, Calcite, Flourite, Beryl, Thulite, Moonstone, Oliveine, Chromite, Unakite, Epidate and Uranium. The festival is sponsored by the Mitchell County Chamber of Commerce. Exhibits - lectures - field trips and night trips for fluorescents. Several gem mines are open to the public for a fee and the visitor may look for his own valuable finds. List of mines may be obtained from the Chamber of Commerce in Spruce Pine.

NORTH CAROLINA RHODODENDRON FESTIVAL. Bakersville. Festival held annually for a long weekend beginning on Wednesday, the third week in June. Festivities include two beauty pagents, square dancing nightly, a golf tournament and running events.

LODGING AND RESTAURANTS
Baker's Motel and Rock Shop. Spruce Pine. "Rockhound Headquarters." Ph: 704/765-9344.
Bakersville Motel. Bakersville. Ph: 765-2647. Open all year.
Peak Mountain Apts. Write P. O. Box 428, Spruce Pine, N. C.
Big Lynn Lodge. Little Switzerland, N. C. 28749. May thru Oct. Ph: 765-4257.
Chalet Motor Lodge. Little Switzerland, N. C. June thru Oct. Ph: 765-2153.
Mountain View Motel. Little Switzerland, N. C. Ph: 765-4233.
Skyline Hotel. Little Switzerland, N. C. May thru Oct.
Oakwood Motel, Spruce Pine, N. C. Ph: 765-6161
Beams, Spruce Pine, N. C. Ph: 765-6191.
Baker's. Spruce Pine, N. C. Ph: 688-2647
Crabtree Meadows Restaurant. Milepost 339.5 Blue Ridge Parkway.
Rhododendron Steak House. Bakersville, N. C.

CRAFT SHOPS
Hensley's Forge. 5 mi. S. Spruce Pine; **Woody's Chair Shop.** 3 mi. S. Spruce Pine; **Thayer Artcrafts.** Marion Rd., Spruce Pine; **Jim Sockwell's Pottery.** Hwy. 226 at Pkwy. Spruce Pine; **Master Craft.** Spruce Pine.

MUSEUM OF NORTH CAROLINA MINERALS
Milepost 331. Blue Ridge Parkway

The Museum is situated near the heart of the Spruce Pine Mineral District. Parkway travelers should stop to get an introduction to the varied mineral resources that are found in North Carolina. The Museum contains exhibits and choice specimens on display. More than 300 varieties.

PENLAND CRAFT SCHOOL
Bakersville Rd., Penland, N. C.

Penland School of Crafts, opened in 1929, recently celebrated its 50th anniversary. One of the oldest and largest of its kind in the United States, the school is dedicated to a serious craft program. From humble beginnings the school has grown to house space and equipment, along with accommodations, for 100 students. All adults with a serious desire to learn are welcome. Modest tuition and some work-study scholarships are available. Both graduate and undergraduate credits may be earned through East Tennessee State University. Courses taught include: weaving, ceramics, metalsmithing, jewelry, photography, enameling, graphics, woodworking, sculpture and glass blowing. For more information write: Penland School, Penland, N. C. 28765. Phone: 704/765-2359.

Roan Mountain   *Courtesy - U.S. Forest Service - Southern Region*

ROAN MOUNTAIN GARDENS. N. C. 261 north of Bakersville, and TN 143 south of Roan Mountain, TN. A part of Pisgah National Forest. This scenic vacation area covers 7,000 acres along top and sides of Roan Mountain, elev. 6,284. Colorful rhododendron gardens cover 600 acres and Fraser fir and spruce cover 850 acres. These gardens occupy the site of the "Cloudland Hotel" built in 1885 by Gen. Thomas Wilder. The hotel burned just before World War I. Visitors are attracted to the natural garden on the mountain's crest which is in full bloom at the end of June. The remarkable flora and unusual plants have attracted botanists from many countries to this mountain. In the 18th century, John Fraser, a noted botanist, reported a new plant found on Roan Mountain—***Rhododendron catawbiense.*** Dr. Asa Gray referred to Roan as "the most beautiful mountain east of the Rockies." Paved roads provide easy access to picnic areas.

POLK COUNTY
Established 1856

COUNTY SEAT: COLUMBUS, *Elevation 1,145 Ft.*
COUNTY POPULATION: *12,984*
PRINCIPAL TOWNS: *Tryon, Columbus, Saluda*
HISTORY: County named in honor of Col. William Polk, Revolutionary officer. In 1844 the General Assembly of North Carolina altered boundary lines and ceded a small portion of Rutherford County; a few years later this strip of land became a part of Polk County. The county seat was named for Dr. Columbus Mills who was instrumental in the formation of the county.

TRYON
U.S. 176—1-26 South of Asheville

Tryon became a prominent resort in the gay ninties: The town and nearby mountain bear the surname of William Tryon, British Governor of the colony of North Carolina in 1765. Located in the thermal belt, Tryon enjoys a marvelous climate. There are long freeze free growing seasons, and when the frosts do come, they are gentle. This unusual condition is due to the temeprature inversions. Also referred to as the Verdant Zone, the width of the belt varies, and there are places where freezes never occur. Scientists have devoted much study to this rarity of nature. Many residents of Tryon have migrated from other parts of the country. Artists, writers, educators and other noted professionals have settled here. Fox hunting, horse shows and the steeplechase have avid support and participation. There are hundreds of miles of marked trails for riding, and many cross beautiful estates. Lush gardens grace the houses belonging to the residents of Tryon; the area is rich in native flora. Camellias, azaleas, and other indigenous plants provide beauty nearly all year.

MUSEUMS
Polk County Historical Museum. 1 Depot St. Ph: 894-8827. Exhibits of Polk County history from the Revolution to the present. Open: Tues.-Thurs. 10 to 12.
Tryon Fine Arts Center. Melrose Ave. Closed summer. Classes and sales for crafts, paintings and jewelry. Center also has **Theatre** and **Art Gallery.**
Tryon Antique Car Museum. Tryon. Ph: 859-9481. 50 year collection of American prestige cars. Summer weekend afternoons only. Other hours by appointment.

INNS AND SHOPS
Pine Crest Inn. 200 Pine Crest Lane. Ph: 859-6800.
Stonehedge Inn. Tryon. Ph: 859-9114.
Iron Horse Guild Crafts. 409 Trade St. Ph: 859-6785.
Valhalla Hand Weavers. US 176 N. Also I-26 N. from Tryon.
Tack Shop. 241 S. Trade St.
Blue Ridge Weavers. S. Trade St.
Year's Ago Antiques. 121 S. Trade St.
The Book Shelf. 218 Pacolet St.
Trade St. Gallery. Tryon.

Blockhouse Steeplechase

BLOCK HOUSE. This old home site is on the lines of four counties and two states. Famous for its beautiful setting and the Block House Steeplechase, which is run on the property each spring — usually in late March. The town really comes alive in a colorful way when the racing silks are flying. The eyecatching white horse on wheels is always in prominent view. Crowds stream into the Block House property on Steeplechase day and may have tail-gate picnics. Exciting and loads of fun.

PEARSON'S FALLS. *U.S. 176. North of Tryon. Watch for signs.* Tryon Garden Club maintains the trails and wild flowers. Stunning nature walk and falls. Be sure to go all the way to the top — climbing is gentle and easy — you will enjoy every minute in the damp, dappled shade. Covered picnic pavilion. Small fee.

RESTAURANTS
Hearthstone Inn Restaurant. US 176 S. Ph: 859-5200.
Caro-Mi Dining Room. US 176 N. Wed. through Sat. Ph: 859-5200.

SALUDA

The stretch of Northland South Carolina traversed by US 176 is geographically and historically the gateway to the Blue Ridge Mountains. Hwy. 176 was completed through the Saluda Gap in the early 1900's, serving as a main artery and supplementing the railroad for tourist travel to the mountains. The area known as the Pacolet Valley is now bypassed by Interstate 26, but it is still beautiful and popular with visitors. Many old homes and inns are still in use, and interesting little shops make Saluda a special place to spend some time. Partial list follows: **Nostalgia Antiques - Danletta Duke's Pottery - Saluda Mountain Crafts - Snaggy Hollow Crafts - Grandma's Attic - Whistle Stop Crafts - Railroad House Restaurant.**

RUTHERFORD COUNTY
Established 1779

COUNTY SEAT: RUTHERFORDTON. *Elevation 1,096 Ft.*
COUNTY POPULATION: *53,787*
VACATION AREAS: *Chimney Rock, Lake Lure*

Situated in the heart of the thermal belt, Rutherford County is steeped in history and tradition. Topography ranges from mountains in the northwest to rolling hills of the east. The western boundary of the county is just west of Chimney Rock. Lake Lure is formed by the tumbling waters of Rocky Broad River. Lake Lure and Chimney Rock play an important part in the recreational life of the county. Many summer cottages and camp grounds serve as focal points for summer activities, and the Lake Lure beach is a gathering place for young people. Fairfield Mountains is a thriving Lake Lure resort community.

HISTORY: Rutherfordton, is the county's oldest town. From the time of its founding in 1765 to the Civil War, it was a frontier town on the edge of the western wilderness. Many noted doctors, lawyers and theologians came to the frontier to begin their profession. For many years it was an educational center and a number of stage coaches reached the town every week. The coming of the railroads in the 1870's did much to spur the county forward.

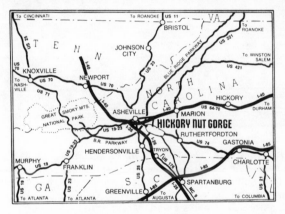

CHIMNEY ROCK — LAKE LURE — BAT CAVE
Southeast of Asheville, U.S. 74 - U.S. 64 - NC 9

The natives call this section "The Gorge," a descriptive name for some of the most dramatic scenery in Western North Carolina. The Gorge refers to the rugged land down the mountain east of Hickory Nut Gap. Sharp heights are crowned by Chimney Rock and the depths are cut by the rushing, tumbling waters of Hickory Creek and Rocky Broad River which empty into Lake Lure. Step off the highway anywhere (U.S. 74 or N.C. 9) and you may fish the Rocky Broad (during fishing season with a license!). The state stocks the streams with rainbow trout. The highway follows the river and is a beautiful drive, with campgrounds, motels, inns, restaurants and small shops.

LAKE LURE

With twenty seven miles of shoreline, stone cliffs and incredible views, Lake Lure has attracted vacationers for years. Curves and coves are dotted with cottages and all the water sports are enjoyed here. Swimming, fishing, water skiing. Boat docks and launching ramps—boats for rent and supplies. Remodeled beach house on 200 yard beach. Buy your fishing license at the hardware store.

BOTTOMLESS POOLS AND WATERFALLS. *Off U.S. 74 at Lake Lure. All year.* This beautiful spot is shared with the public for a very small fee.

RESTAURANTS   **ESMERALDA INN.** Chimney Rock
THE STONE HEARTH. Bat Cave   **DUCK CEDAR INN.** Lake Lure

Photo: Chimney Rock Park

CHIMNEY ROCK PARK. U.S. 74; 25 miles southeast of Asheville. Open March thru Nov. Daily. Entrance fee and group rates. Chimney Rock has been a great attraction in this area since it was opened to the public in 1912. Privately owned, the park contains over 1,000 acres of unspoiled natural wonders—Opera Box, Devil's Head, Moonshiner's Cave and Spectacular Hickory Nut Falls (twice the height of Niagara) cascading to the valley below. The chimney is a geological wonder of solid granite. The gigantic monolith stands apart from the mountain about 1,000 feet above the level of the gorge. Ride the 258 foot elevator carved through the center of the rock; from the overlook you will have a spectacular 75 mile view of the mountains, cliffs and Lake Lure. Wear safe shoes for the nature trails and rock climbing. Walking trails lead to Hickory Nut Falls overlooking the Gorge. SKY LOUNGE RESTAURANT, snack bar and souvenirs on top of the rock. Visit CHIMNEY ROCK GALLERIES, featuring unusual gift items - small furniture, brass, some antiques, candy, crystal, paintings, stuffed toys and dolls. Overlooking roaring Rocky Broad River. At park entrance. *

MOUNTAIN VIEW CRAFT VILLAGE. Under development. Ride sky lift to the village. Daily unlimited rides for small fee. Opposite Chimney Rock.

*adv.

Chimney Rock Park (704)625-9611
PO Box 39 (800)277-9611
Chimney Rock NC 28720

SWAIN COUNTY
Established 1871

COUNTY SEAT: BRYSON CITY. *Elevation 1,736 Ft.*
COUNTY POPULATION: *10,283*
PRINCIPAL PLACES: *Bryson City, Great Smoky Mountains National Park, Fontana Lake, Fontana Dam, Nantahala River, Cherokee Indian Reservation.*

The recreational aspects of Swain County have attracted millions of visitors. A large part of the county is located in the Great Smoky Mountains National Park and the Cherokee Indian Reservation is nearby, northeast of Bryson City. Over 21,000 acres of the Nantahala National Forest are in the county. Visitors will find fishing in Fontana Lake, numerous streams and rivers. Deer and bear hunting are both popular, and there are vast areas suitable for camping and picnicking. Some of the most challenging whitewater canoeing can be experienced on the Nantahala River. Swain County is served by the Interstate Highway system. I-26, I-40 and US 19, US 19A and US 441 connect the county with major cities. US 441 brings over 16 million visitors a year. Swain County was established in 1871 and named after David Lowrie Swain, Governor of North Carolina.

BRYSON CITY INNS: *

HEMLOCK INN. *U.S. 19, Bryson City, N.C. 704/488-9820.* Opens early May to early November. Mr. and Mrs. John Shell own and operate this simple but charming country Inn on top of a mountain. There are twenty five rooms in the Inn and four cottages with kitchens. This quiet retreat serves outstanding food, but the dining room (seating 60) can usually accommodate guests only. Early in the season you might get lucky and make reservations for dinner. *Directions: U.S. 19 to 19A. Exit Hyatt Creek Road—proceed until you turn back to U.S. 19. Turn left two miles and look for sign. Write: Hemlock Inn, Bryson City, N.C. 28713.*

FRYEMONT INN. *Fryemont Road, Bryson City. (704) 488-2159, "The Inn Unique".* In business 60 years, Fryemont Inn sits on a hill overlooking the town, wonderfully located for area activities. Thirty seven rooms, private baths. Dining room serving family style, three meals, Monday-Friday. No lunch sat. and Sun.

FRYE-RANDOLPH HOUSE. *Fryemont Road, Bryson City. (704) 488-3472.* Open all year. Constructed as a home around 1895, this small old fashioned country inn is furnished with antiques and seems secluded in the heart of town. Delightful food, varied menu. Breakfast and dinner daily. Open to public by reservations.

NANTAHALA GORGE
   a) Ferebee Memorial Site. U.S. 19   b) Canoe Launch Area. U.S. 19

NANTAHALA OUTDOOR CENTER. *U.S. 19 at Wesser. Thirteen miles south of Bryson City.* 8 mile guided raft trips through the scenic Nantahala Gorge. Exciting three hour trip. Restaurant and motel. Fully stocked outfitters store with white water gear, groceries, books. Complete safety oriented instruction program.   Write: Nantahala Outdoor Outdoor Center, Inc., Star Rt. Box 68, Bryson City, N. C. 28713. Phone: (704) 488-6407.

Looking Glass   *Courtesy - Asheville Chamber of Commerce*

TRANSYLVANIA COUNTY
Established 1861

COUNTY SEAT: BREVARD. *Elevation 2,230 Ft.*
COUNTY POPULATION: *23,417*
COMMUNITIES: *Brevard, Rosman, Lake Toxaway*
  Southwest of Asheville on US 64 and 276.

The origin of the name of Transylvania comes from Latin words meaning across the woods. The county was appropriately named. Within its borders are 83,000 acres of the Pisgah National Forest and over 5,000 acres of the Nantahala National Forest. Transylvania contains the headwaters of the French Broad River. Beginning with four large tributaries, the waters join at Rosman, creating the main stream which flows on a northerly route through Western North Carolina into Tennessee. A vacation spot supreme, Transylvania is known as the land of the waterfalls. It contains the Cradle of Forestry and other Pisgah Forest attractions. Hundreds of young people enjoy the county's summer camps, and music lovers are thrilled by summer concerts at Brevard Music Center. Adding to the economy are Brevard Junior College, a thriving retirement community and two of North Carolina's most prominent industries, Du Pont (x-ray film division) and Olin (fine paper and film division).

HISTORY: Transylvania County was formed in 1861 just at the outbreak of the Civil War, from parts of Henderson and Jackson Counties. Transylvania lands that had been traversed by well worn Indian trails were occupied as early as the late 1700's when western lands were opened up by the state of North Carolina. The richness of the soil and the abundance of game attracted early settlers. However, the dispute over borders delayed the formation of the county. Brevard was established near the home of W.P. Poor, and was named for Ephraim Brevard secretary of the Mecklenburg convention. For more information:

Brevard Chamber of Commerce
35 W. Main St. P. O. Box 589
Brevard, NC 28712
(704) 883-3700

BREVARD

Brevard Music Festival   Photo — N.C. Travel and Tourism Division

BREVARD MUSIC CENTER. 884-2011 and summer box office: 884-2019. Probart St. off Caldwell St., "The summer cultural center of the South." Transylvania orchestra student and faculty performances, guests artists and opera, symphony concerts, pop concerts. One of the five major Music Festivals in the U.S. First week in July thru middle of August. Seats reserved for weekend concerts. Season tickets available. Write: Brevard Music Center, P. O. Box 592, Brevard, N. C. 28712.

SHOPS AND RESTAURANTS *
CHEESE WEDGE AND KEG. Corner U.S. 64 and McLean Road, next to Northwestern Bank, Brevard. (704) 884-4050. A country store with some of our favorite things. Rocking chairs, and crafts. Fine cheese and wine (domestic and imported), and specialty foods. Take out orders and picnic baskets.
THE SOUP KETTLE in adjoining log cabin. Tasty lunch. 11 a.m. - 2:30 p.m. Mon.-Sat.

LAURA'S RESTAURANT. U.S. 64. Between Brevard and Toxaway. (704) 966-4885. Open all year. 11 a.m.-9 p.m. Closed Wed. Enjoy marvelous meals in this cozy rustic log cabin. Dine on open or screened porch. Fireside dining on cool nights. Family restaurant featuring four entrees, fresh vegetables, homemade desserts. Sunday dinner a special treat. Reservations.

 **The Red Barn**

RED BARN GIFT AND COFFEE SHOP. U.S. 64. (704) 966-4325. Open June through Oct. Mon.-Sat. 10-5. Lunch served 12-2. Desserts all day. Red Barn is noted for Bernice's pastries, unusual gifts, crafts and cookbooks. Located near Lake Toxaway. Favorite stopping place between Cashiers and Brevard.

* adv.

TRANSYLVANIA RESTAURANTS

RED LION INN. *Hwy. 178. 3½ miles south of Rosman. (704) 862-4491.* Open all year. Mon.-Sat. 6 p.m.-10 p.m. Earlier during music festival. Take a pretty country drive to this rustic inn by a stream. Specializing in choice aged steaks, seafood and mountain trout. Homemade breads and desserts. French onion soup. Entertainment Fri. and Sat. Brownbagging. Master Charge and Visa.

For Rent: Four Inn guest rooms with private bath. Continental breakfast served. Moderate price. Four housekeeping cabins for rent by night, week or month. *

THE PINES COUNTRY INN. *Rt. 2. Hart Rd., (704) 877-3131. Between Brevard and Hendersonville. Turn off U.S. 64 to Holmes State Forest Rd.* At little River Community-Baptist Church-take Cascade Lake Rd. to Hart Rd. This is the real thing - an old country inn overlooking a serene valley. Pick your room - mine is the one with the upstairs porch. Built as a home around 1886, the Pines has operated as an Inn since 1905. You will enjoy the slow pace and personal attention. Twelve acres, inn and cottages, rooms for 50 guests. Breakfast and dinner included and served family style. Mon. - Sat. and Sunday noon. Outside guests for meals by reservation. *

The Red Door. Restaurant. U.S. 64 near Sapphire and Cashiers.
The Picnic Basket. 34 South Broad St., Brevard
Greylogs Restaurant. U.S. 276, Caesar's Head, S. C.
Pisgah Fish Camp. Restaurant, U.S. 276 and N.C. 280

HIGHLAND BOOKS. *409 Broad St. 884-2424. Shopping center, U.S. 64 near Brevard College.* Well-stocked book store with a good selection of regional books, maps and field guides.

MORRIS GIFT SHOP. *5 West Main St. 883-2175.* Out-of-town newspapers. Also books, paperbacks, cards and gifts.

BILTMORE DAIRY BAR. *U.S. 64, Brevard.* Ice cream emporium. No sandwiches, but that good and famous Biltmore ice cream. A favorite stop for campers.

SHERWOOD FOREST: Cedar Mountain, N.C. (704) 885-2091
A resort/year round community on U.S. 276, eight miles south of Brevard.

The residential community enjoys great natural beauty in its surroundings. Sherwood Forest offers the ideal setting for nature lovers. There are 1000 (plus) acres, five stocked lakes, streams, nature trails, large heated pool, hot tub, tennis courts and shuffleboard. Sherwood Forest justifiably boasts of having the most beautiful Executive Par 3 golf course in the southeast. The community, established in 1957, has many choice large lots for sale as well as a condominium planned unit development. Rental cottages and condominium units are available weekly, monthly or weekends. Gift shop with crafts, but no restaurant. Write: Mr. Arthur M. Dehon, Jr., P.O. Box 156, Cedar Mountain, NC 28718. *

Sliding Rock   *Photo - U.S. Forest Service*

PISGAH AND NANTAHALA NATIONAL FORESTS
IN TRANSYLVANIA COUNTY

CRADLE OF FORESTRY. *U.S. 276, 10 mi. from Pisgah Ranger Station.* The birthplace of American forestry. The first school of forestry began in 1898 on part of George Vanderbilt's estate called "Pisgah Forest." Founded by Dr. Carl Schenck, summer classes were held at the Biltmore Forest School campus. The "campus" consisted of rustic cabins and farm houses in the old "Pink Beds" community. Outstanding contributions were made in the field of Forestry. Campus tour includes: School House, Commissary, Ranger's Dwelling, Dr. Schenck's office, Black Forest Lodge, Blacksmith Shop, Student Quarters, "Hell Hole," Logging train exhibit. No charge! Visitor Center.

SLIDING ROCK. *Off U.S. 276. Late May through Labor Day. All day till dark.* Each year hundreds of campers and visitors brave the cold waters of Looking Glass Creek for an exciting "dunking" at the bottom of Sliding Rock. Because of the popularity of the rock, a handsome new stone and cedar bathhouse has been built for convenience and comfort. Other additions: improved gravel paths—stone steps—two observation platforms above and below the falls. No fee for this fun! 60 ft. sliding area.

DAVIDSON RIVER CAMPGROUND. *U.S. 276 north of Brevard. Off 276 at Schenck Job Corps entrance.* An 84 foot swinging bridge spans the Davidson River to provide a better entrance to the popular Art Loeb Trail for hiking. Parking area.

LOOKING GLASS FALLS. 5 miles from intersections of U.S. 276, U.S. 64 *and N.C. 280.* One of the most scenic and best known falls in Eastern U.S. Picturesque and unbroken rush of water 30 ft. wide and 60 ft. high. Massive rock towers above falls. Parking near falls. 4 miles from Ranger Station.

PISGAH RANGER STATION. *PISGAH FOREST. 2 miles NW of intersection N.C. 280 and U.S. 276.* Open all year. (704) 877-3265. Open 7 days a week June through Labor Day. Office and Visitor Center.

PISGAH ECOLOGY TRAIL. *45 minute tour behind Ranger Station.* Self-guided tapes available. Ask for permit to Shining Rock Wilderness.

WHITE WATER FALLS SCENIC AREA. *At Sapphire. U.S. 64 turn south on N.C. 1149.* Whitewater River drops over 400 feet. Spectacular series of falls and cascades. Picnicking, overlooks, parking areas.

Transylvania Co.

Camp Kahdalea   Photo - Jack Gwennap

CAMP KAHDALEA FOR GIRLS. *Camp Kahdalea Road, off US 64, 6 miles southwest of Brevard.* A private summer camp for girls, 7-16, offering a full program of watersports (also water skiing), landsports, tennis, horseback riding, art, drama, music, backpacking and white water canoeing. The property is adjacent to the Pisgah National Forest. A strong emphasis is placed on Christian growth and character building, mental, social and physical development. Sessions include a Three Week Term in June and July and a Five Week Term in July and August. The camper-staff ratio is four to one and enrollment is limited to approximately one hundred campers. Kahdalea is owned and operated by Mr. & Mrs. Walter Montgomery Oates who reside year round at the camp. ·

TOXAWAY

LAKE TOXAWAY. *U.S. 64.* A residential resort community described as the Switzerland of America, surrounding North Carolina's largest, private recreational lake. Rental cottages. Golf, boating, tennis. Lake Toxaway is 20 miles west of Brevard, 15 miles east of Cashiers.

TOXAWAY FALLS. 20 miles south of Brevard on U.S. 64. Highway crosses 123 ft. high falls. Hike *carefully* down to pools at bottom to fish—camp—swim.

CONNESTEE FALLS. *U.S. 276 six miles south of Brevard.* Two falls from Connestee and Batson Creeks, each about 110 feet high. Well kept overlook and trails.

WATERFALLS. More than 100 waterfalls in area, located on North Fork of the French Broad River, West Fork, South Mills River, Bear Wallow Creek and scores of streams. Detailed map available: Chamber of Commerce, Brevard, N.C. 28712.

MORGAN MILL. *Kahdalea Camp Road.* The ultimate in antiques! "The old-fashioned ways" are still used to grind corn in a picturesque 1856 mill. Mill wheel two stories high and 30 feet in diameter harnesses the strength of a mountain stream. Truly something to see. *5 mi. s.w. of Brevard off U.S. 64.*

112

WATAUGA COUNTY
Created 1849

COUNTY SEAT: *BOONE.*
COUNTY POPULATION: *31,678*
ELEVATION: *3266 Ft.*
INCORPORATED TOWNS: *Boone, Blowing Rock, Seven Devils*

EARLY HISTORY: An Indian word meaning *"Whispering Waters"* named the county. Several Indian tribes had occupied this area for long years before it was vacated by the Cherokee Tribe and gradually opened up to make way for white men. The earliest known white visitor was the Moravian religious leader Bishop August Spangenberg who came in 1752 and later led his colony to settle in the Piedmont. A road cut through the region to Tennessee was used by Daniel Boone in the 1760's. Boone hunted the territory and spent time in a cabin located on the present day campus of Appalachian State University. James Robertson later used the same track to lead settlers into the district. After the Confiscation Act, land was transferred from the English Earl of Granville to the State of North Carolina. Settlers from northern states came into the region and Watauga County was created. Covering 320 square miles, Watauga County has four river system headwaters: ***The Watauga River, New River, Catawba and Yadkin.*** There are many clear streams and waterfalls, hardwood forests and rugged terrain. Steep valleys range from 3,000 to 3,700 feet. High meadows resemble parts of Switzerland. Boone is the home of Appalachian State University and is also an industrial community. Blowing Rock, chartered in 1889 with an elevation of 3,579, is largely a resort community and for years has welcomed summer visitors who have come to escape the heat of the lowlands. Seven Devils was incorporated in 1979 and has only 47 year round residents. The area has now developed a large ski industry and visitors come year round.

BOONE CRAFTSMEN'S FESTIVAL

Over seventy craftsmen participate in this festival held annually in August and October at Holiday Inn Conference Center, Boone. Some of the highest quality craftsmanship in the nation is demonstrated at these fairs. Continuing for several days, the event includes musical entertainment. Presented by Blue Ridge Hearthside Crafts, Asso. *Write: Box 1388, Boone, N.C. 28607.*

HORN IN THE WEST

An outstanding historical drama - the story of Daniel Boone -presented in a beautiful amphitheatre. *Nightly except Mondays during July and August.* Don't miss this colorful drama as it unfolds history, romance, music, comedy and battle on three stages. While on the grounds, visit the Daniel Boone Gardens. Group discount rates available upon request.

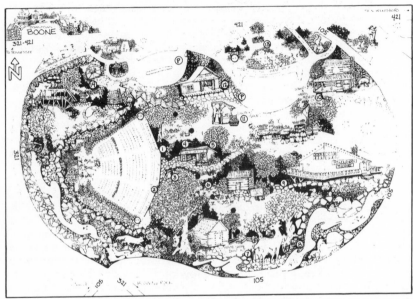

Horn in the West

EXCITING OUTDOOR DRAMA AND MORE!

1. Horn in the West
2. RAIN SHELTERS
3. CONCESSION STAND
4. TICKET OFFICE
5. ADMINISTRATIVE OFFICE
6. TATUM CABIN

7. NATE SHOPE SCOUT HUT
8. NATURE TRAIL
9. POWDERHORN THEATRE
10. STANLEY A HARRIS SR. MUSEUM OF SCOUTING
11. FARMERS MARKET

12. DAN'L BOONE GEN'L STORE
13. DAN'L BOONE OVERLOOK
14. DANIEL BOONE NATIVE GARDENS
15. RESTROOMS
16. PARKING

● PICNIC AREAS

GOLF

BOONE GOLF COURSE. *Off US 321-221 in Boone. Open to public, 8 am until dark. Cart rentals. Ph: 264-8760.*
WILLOW CREEK GOLF COURSE. 3½ miles south of Boone off US 105. Daily 8 am until dark. 9 hole course. Cart rentals and pull carts. Ph: 963-4025.

RESTAURANTS:

DANIEL BOONE INN. *105 Hardin St. Ph: 264-8657.*
MARVIN'S GARDENS. *240 East King St. Ph: 262-1208.*

Courtesy - Appalachian State University

APPALACHIAN STATE UNIVERSITY
Boone, N.C. 28608

Founded in 1899 as Watauga Academy, Appalachian State University is located in the heart of the Blue Ridge Mountains, close to the borders of Virginia and Tennessee. Now a part of the consolidated University of North Carolina, the campus occupies 48 buildings on a 75 acre main campus. Several new buildings are on the new 180 acre west campus. The enrollment is 10,000 students. Appalachian maintains two campuses away from Boone for experimental studies.

THE CENTER FOR CONTINUING EDUCATION. Courses for adult students. Center hosts meetings for state, regional, national and international organizations. Some areas of study include agriculture, medicine, science, business and law. Special courses are designed to assist in chosen vocations and daily living. The Center also provides lodging, dining and meeting facilities.

HOWARD W. MAST, INC. *N. C. 194 Valle Crucis. Between Banner Elk and Vilas. 963-4711.* Daily except Sunday. How can we tell you about the Mast store? You just must see this unbelievable old building. Opened in 1898, it

was originally stocked with such items as calico, men's hats, wash boards and hand plows. You'll love the authentic old posters advertising merchandise from another era. Current stock has everything from horse collars to hominy grits. Entered on the National Register of Historic Places.

115

BLOWING ROCK

HISTORY OF BLOWING ROCK: In 1889 Blowing Rock was incorporated as the highest town in North Carolina. Situated on the Eastern Continental Divide and enjoying an elevation of 4,200 feet, Blowing Rock became a popular summer resort. With increased interest in travel to mountain areas, hotels, inns and boarding houses became a primary business in the late 1800's. Access was not easy, but eager vacationers came by train to Lenoir and traveled by carriage and wagon up the Lenoir Turnpike to the cool air of the mountains. A 4,090 foot cliff called Blowing Rock overhangs the Johns River Gorge. Sheer rock walls form a flume and when the wind sweeps down, a strong force is created; a light object will blow back after it is thrown. This astonishing creation of nature is worth your exploration. It is beautifully landscaped and on a clear day you will see many distant mountains.

ATTRACTIONS

Credit: National Park Service

MOSES H. CONE MEMORIAL PARK. *Blue Ridge Parkway. Blowing Rock Hwys. 221-321.* The park is operated and maintained as a unit of the Blue Ridge Parkway administered by U.S. Dept.of Interior—National Park Service. It is one of 11 such areas along the Parkway and covers 3,600 acres. Originally the mountain estate of Mr. and Mrs. Moses H. Cone, it was first named Flat Top Manor and was built at the turn of the century. It was deeded to the Federal government in 1950 by the Moses H. Cone Memorial Hospital, Greensboro, N.C.

THE PARKWAY CRAFT CENTER. *Cone Memorial Park, Blue Ridge Parkway. 9 a.m to 5:30, May to November.* A shop sponsored by the Southern Highland Handicraft Guild for its member-craftsmen. Baskets, cone-craft, woodcarving, furniture, brooms, rugs, pottery, weaving, iron work, copper, enamels, silver jewelry, dolls. Visit the Frances L. Goodrich Pioneer Museum while here.

Green Park Inn - (c.1882)

GREEN PARK INN. Open all year and ideal for summer or winter vacation. 80 rooms recently restored to new elegance. Relax in the Divide Lounge and then enjoy the charming formal dining room. Boutique and Beauty Salon. Newly built condominiums will be available summer 1981. Victorian style architecture - spacious-exclusive. For information write: Green Park Realy Co., P. O. Box 28605, Blowing Rock, N. C.*

Green Park Inn. Lenoir Turnpike U.S. 321 (704) 295-3141.

LODGING—SHOPS

HOUND EARS LODGE AND CLUB. *Hwy. 105 between Linville and Boone. Ph.: 704/963-4321. Large double bedrooms and suites. Villas - all have private balconys and views. Some houses for rent through Lodge. Excellent dining room. Golf - Ski. Must have reservations. Write: Hound Ears Lodge and Club, Box 188, Blowing Rock, N.C. 28605.*

LAMP POST ANTIQUES. *Main St., Ph.: 295-3868.*
NEEDLE-NICELY. *Main St., Ph.: 295-3313.*
GOODWIN GUILD WEAVERS. *W. Cornish Rd. Ph: 295-3577.*

RESTAURANTS

WINSTON'S. *Sunset Drive. Ph.: 295-7391.*
CONTINENTAL DIVIDE RESTAURANT-CAFE. *Main St. Ph.: 295-3777.*
COFFEY'S. *US 321 Bypass. Ph.: 295-3030.*
FARM HOUSE RESTAURANT. *S. Main St. Ph.: 295-7361.*

Watauga Co.

Photo - W.M. Cline of Asheville

TWEETSIE RAILROAD. *U.S. 321-221 three miles north of Blowing Rock.* The train trip through Indian country is exciting and noisy, but this attraction is not the only treat in store when you take the small fry. A professional magic show performed at regular intervals in the Tweetsie Palace Theatre is marvelous. Live orchestra plays accompaniment and a saloon type bar, reminiscent of other days, furnishes the refreshment. A double chair lift takes you up to a mine where you may pan for treasure or ride into the mouse mine to watch animated animals extracting their golden cheese from underground. A bus ride up for those who do not care to take the chair lift. Tweetsie continues to add interest and variety to its many attractions. New to many visitors will be a shooting gallery, a display of antique steam engines, an old timey firehouse with horse drawn fire engines and a recreated Indian Village. A one price park, your entrance fee entitles you to all the attractions. Picnic areas and locker for your baskets. *

BLOWING ROCK HORSE SHOW
Broyhill Park — July — Hwy. 221
The oldest continuous horse show in America. A formal show — attracts an enormous number of people from all over the country. Horse show weekend fills the town and everything is crowded. Plan ahead.

TROUT FISHING
Stocked Lakes: Tater Hill Lake north of Boone, Trout Lake in Cone Park, Price Lake and Sims Pond on the Parkway.
Stocked Streams: Winklers Creek, Gashen Creek, Middle Fork, Upper Watauga River.
Pay for what you catch: Watauga Trout Ponds near Tumbling Rock on Hwy. 105 and "Pay-Day" Trout Farm 4 miles from Blowing Rock off Shull's Mill Road.

* adv.

YANCEY COUNTY
Established 1833

COUNTY SEAT: Burnsville. *Elevation 2,817 Ft.*
COUNTY POPULATION: *14,934*
COMMUNITIES: *Burnsville, Celo, Micaville.*

Yancey County is famous for Mt. Mitchell (elev. 6,684), the highest peak in the Appalachians and in eastern America. A county of unparalled beauty, Yancey attracts world famous artists, musicians, craftsmen, and businessmen. It is a favorite summer resort. Many peaks in the Black Mountains soar over 6,000 feet — Mt. Craig, Big Tom, Balsam Cone, Cattail Peak, etc. With 36,000 acres of the Pisgah National Forest, Mt. Mitchell State Park and the Blue Ridge Parkway, Yancey offers unlimited opportunities for recreation. For more information: *Yancey County Chamber of Commerce, Burnsville, N.C. 28714. (704) 682-7413. Pisgah National Forest — Toecane Ranger District: District Ranger, U.S. Forest Service, P.O. Box 128, Burnsville, N.C. 28714. (704) 682-6146. (On U.S. 19-By-pass in Burnsville.)*

EARLY HISTORY. Settlers began to move up the Toe and Cane River Valleys in the late 1700's. Hardy pioneers seeking land offering hunting, fishing and the promise of good agriculture began to carve out small settlements in the folds of the high mountains. In 1833, Yancey County was formed from Buncombe and Burke and named in honor of Bartlett Yancey, North Carolina member of U.S. Congress. Burnsville was selected as the county seat and named for Captain Otway Burns, an officer in the Navy during the second war with England.

BURNSVILLE
Thirty-seven miles northeast of Asheville via
US 19 — US 19E. US 19W — NC 80

ANNUAL EVENTS
MT. MITCHELL CRAFTS FESTIVAL. *On the Square in Burnsville. First weekend in August.* Sponsored by Yancey County Chamber of Commerce. Mountain crafts, music and barbecue. A big event and lots of fun.

PARKWAY PLAYHOUSE. *Summer theater, July and August.* Produced by University of North Carolina at Greensboro.

PAINTING IN THE MOUNTAINS. Summer session July and August. Fall session in October. Individual instruction in a group setting for beginners and advanced students. Sixteenth season. Reservations: Painting in the Mountains, P. O. Box 903, Burnsville, NC 28714.

MUSIC IN THE MOUNTAINS. Fridays at 7:30 p.m. - July - early August. First Presbyterian Church, Burnsville or United Methodist Church, Spruce Pine. Summer chamber music series. Call for location 682-7215. Honorary director, Mme. Lili Kraus.

INNS and RESTAURANTS

Photo - Brian Westveer

NU-WRAY INN. *On the Square. (704)682-2329.* One of North Carolina's most famous inns and a landmark in Burnsville, the Nu-Wray was built before 1833. It has been operated by the same family for four generations in the tradition of southern hospitality. Period furniture, comfortable bedrooms, and famous food served family-style are well known features. Breakfast daily, supper weekdays only and Sunday mid-day dinner. Call for reservations. *

YANCEY COUNTY COUNTRY STORE. *On the Square. (704) 682-6413.* An old standby with a new look, the country store is a must for every visitor in Yancey County. You will enjoy the look of nostalgia and a wide variety of items. Old fashioned candies, traditional mountain crafts, hiker's maps and guides, regional books. *
THE FEED ROOM. *Open all year.* A charming restuarant and great addition to Yancey County Country Store. Everything prepared from scratch: homemade breads and soups, steaks, trout, fresh vegetables, quiches, and desserts. Serving lunch and dinner every day. Delicious food at old-fashioned prices. *

ROCKING CHAIR INN. *West Main St. Burnsville. (704) 682-2112. April through November.* A rustic mountain guest inn for carefree vacationing. This is a small inn with personalized attention and all comforts. Spacious rooms, private baths, cable color TV. Card room, lounge. Shelter for evening barbecues. Good southern style cooking. Three meals a day. Two dining rooms. Vacation planning and reservations made for area events. Your hosts, Bill and Marjorie Carr. *

* adv.

Mt. Mitchell Golf Course   **Photo - Yancey County Journal**

A VERY SPECIAL MOUNTAIN RESORT *

ALPINE VILLAGE. A new time sharing community with luxuriously furnished two bedroom Chalets that are sold by the week. Breath taking views, tennis, pool, sauna, etc. Model and office: *(704) 675-5911.*

MOUNT MITCHELL GOLF CLUB. Championship 18 hole course recently given honorable mention in top 20 golf courses in North Carolina. Bent grass greens and suprisingly flat for a mountain course. Daily fee play. *(704) 675-4923.*

ALBERT'S BAVARIAN RESTAURANT. Authentic German food served with old world charm, each table overlooking golf course and Mount Mitchell. *Open for breakfast and dinner. For reservations call: (704) 675-4691.*

ALBERT'S GOLF LODGE. A small, modern motel with each room overlooking golf course and mountains. *(704) 675-5011.* Adjacent to ALBERT'S BAVARIAN RESTAURANT.

HOMESITES AND GOLF COURSE TOWN HOUSES FOR SALE. Inquire at ALPINE VILLAGE office or at MOUNT MITCHELL GOLF CLUB.
Location: NC Rt. 80, 16 miles southeast of Burnsville, N.C. or leave Blue Ridge Parkway at Buck Creek Gap and travel 2 miles west on NC Rt. 80 Mail address: Alpine Village, Rt. 80, Burnsville, NC 28714

Yancey Co.

OUTDOOR RECREATION

Carolina Hemlock Campground

Photo - Yancey County Journal

CAROLINA HEMLOCK. *Off NC 80. South of Burnsville.* Favorite recreation area with scenic views and mountain stream. Camping. Swimming (bathouse). Picnic pavillion.

BLACK MOUNTAIN CAMPGROUND. *NC 80 south of Burnsville to Forest Road 472.* Developed campground. Amphitheater. Hiking, fishing, bicycle trail.

MT. MITCHELL STATE PARK. *Accessible only by Blue Ridge Parkway, Milepost 355.4 and NC 128.* Established in 1915 the park covers 1,469 acres and extends along the ridges of the Black Mountains. Campgrounds, trails, picnic shelter, lookout tower, restaurant and lounge. For more information: *Mt. Mitchell State Park, Rt. 5, Box 700, Burnsville, N.C. (704)675-4611.* **NEW MUSEUM**.

HISTORY OF MOUNT MITCHELL. *Elevation 6,684 Ft.* Mt. Mitchell was named for Dr. Elisha Mitchell (1793-1857), a minister and professor of Chemistry, Minerology, and Geology at the University of North Carolina. His dramatic story is as intriguing as the mountain. Dr. Mitchell was born in Connecticut, but his profession brought him to the south and he was drawn to the mountains by his scientific curiosity and the speculations of other scientists. Andre Michaux, renowned French Botanist, had visited the Black Mountains in 1794. Because of the vegetation found there, he believed that the highest peaks in eastern America were in this region. Dr. Mitchell carefully explored and measured elevations over a period of years. His measurement of 1844 determined that the highest peak in the Black Mountains and in eastern America was Mt. Mitchell. His claim was challenged by Senator Thomas Lanier Clingman, and in June, 1857, Dr. Mitchell attempted to survey the mountain again. This was to be his last trip. On a late June afternoon Dr. Mitchell left to hike across the mountain to visit Big Tom Wilson, guide, and hunter of renown. Mitchell did not reach Big Tom and never returned to camp. Hundreds of people searched for him but the mountain skills of Tom Wilson led the search party to Dr. Mitchell's body at the foot of a waterfall. Dr. Mitchell was buried in Asheville, but a year later his body was returned to the mountain which bears his name.

Factory Stores
Outlets
Discount Shops

Outlet shopping in the Carolinas is a great pastime. Many manufacturers of furniture, clothing, textiles and household accessories form the backbone of industry and the economy. We are fortunate that numerous companies offer their products at great savings through Factory Stores, Outlets, and Discount Shops. In this section we list some information which will help you with **Bargain Buying** for **Inflation Living**. This is a selected list; there are other booklets that list all of the outlets. **Round the Mountains** has enlarged this section because we live in a world of mobility. Interstate highways whisk us across the state, and without some planning, we could miss those fun and profitable stops that make the trip worthwhile and exciting. Doesn't everyone love a bargain? Plan a shopping trip to some of the places we suggest!

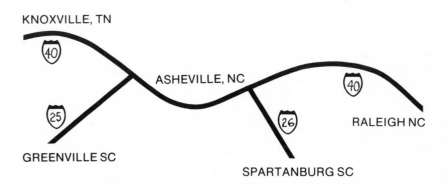

KNOXVILLE, TN

ASHEVILLE, NC

RALEIGH NC

GREENVILLE SC

SPARTANBURG SC

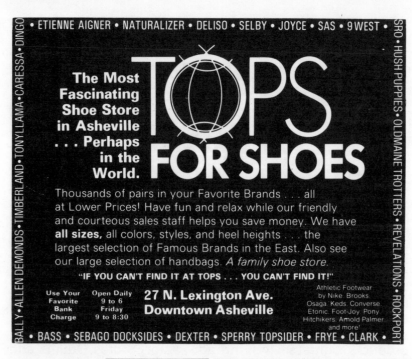

Division of
Dalton Industries, Inc.
FACTORY STORE

Coxe Avenue, Asheville, N.C. 28801
Directions: Hadley is located in downtown Asheville.
Coxe Avenue runs between Patton Avenue and U.S. 25.

FAMOUS HADLEY FASHIONS AT
LOW FACTORY STORE PRICES.

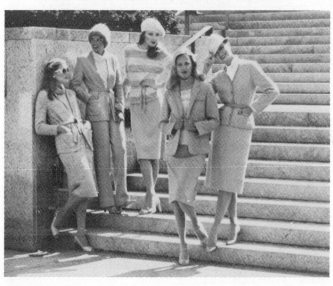

At the Hadley Factory Store you'll find the quality merchandise. Ladies sweaters of cashmere, camel hair and other luxury yarns. Also, beautifully designed coordinated skirts and slacks. Select from better dresses tailored from fine natural yarns as well as easy-care polyester. Plus, you can choose from an assortment of Hadley sports-minded coordinates, designed for the woman who wants to dress for the game — and the gallery.

PHONE 258-1516

FREE PARKING,
MAJOR CREDIT CARDS
ACCEPTED

Open all year
Monday - Saturday

May - October
10 a.m. - 5:30 p.m.

November - April
10 a.m. - 5:00 p.m.

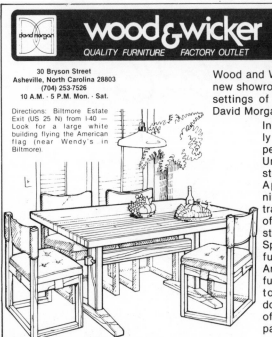

Manufacturers of Solid Pine

Gifts & Decorative Accessories

Visit our Factory Outlet Store
and choose from our complete line of
beautifully crafted solid pine
Household Accessories
and Framed Prints

252-6046

Open 10-5:30, Mon. thru Sat.; and, April thru Dec., 1-6 Sunday

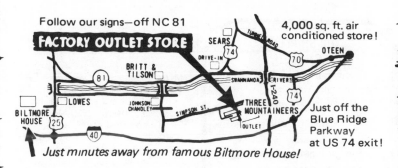

Follow our signs—off NC 81

4,000 sq. ft. air conditioned store!

Just off the Blue Ridge Parkway at US 74 exit!

Just minutes away from famous Biltmore House!

THREE MOUNTAINEERS, INC.

30 Simpson Street, Asheville, North Carolina 28803

This shop is worth the search. Terrific bargains in reproductions of early American decorative items. Framed prints, small tables, luggage racks and lamps are among hundreds of items. Candles and soaps. Kitchen and bath accessories, wall cabinets, spice racks, mirrors. And a note of cheer for the energy crunch, Three Mountaineers has a new product—Mountaineer Fire Logs made from pressed wood—also kindling wood. Firelogs are a special bargain in the summer!

127

Open Mon-Sat 9:30-5:00
Phone (704) 686-5445

BEACON OUTLET STORE, Whitson Ave., off U.S. 70, Swannanoa, NC
Mon.-Sat., 9:30 to 5:00 p.m. (704) 686-5445. Take Swannanoa Exit #59 from I-40. Located east of Asheville in the stone building behind NCNB Bank, you'll find fantastic bargains in blankets, sheets, towels and spreads. Shop in comfort and select from a wide variety of home fashions, everything from matching spreads and draperies to table mats, linens and other bedroom, bath and kitchen items, as well as beach blankets, sheet blankets, throw rugs and bath sets. Beacon is the world's largest manufacturer of blankets; you will find a wonderful selection for gifts or personal use and a good supply of infant and youth blankets. Beacon is now a part of Cannon Mills Co. and carries many of the Cannon fashion products. A popular outlet in the Asheville area!

LONDONTOWN FACTORY-OUTLET STORE
Save ½ Off Conventional Store Prices
NATIONALLY FAMOUS MEN'S AND WOMEN'S
RAINCOATS • JACKETS • LEATHERS • OUTERWEAR
SLACKS • CURRENT SEASON STYLES

Irregulars and Broken Size Lots
Also ask to see our children's outerwear.

Located in Asheville, North Carolina
Off I-240 - Westgate/Hilton Exit
Accessible via I-26 and I-40.

WESTGATE SHOPPING CENTER
WESTGATE PARKWAY
VISA*   **(704) 258-8123**   master charge

Store Hours: Monday - Saturday 10 a.m. to 9 p.m.

Visit our other WYTHEVILLE, VA. SCRANTON, PA. BRATTLEBORO, VT.
stores in SIKESTON, MO. HANCOCK, MD.

WHITE SHIELD FACTORY OUTLET
Bedding and Household Linens
SAVINGS 20% - 50%

109 W. Main St., Hazelwood, N. C.
(Just off 19-A - Waynesville By-pass)

Mon.-Sat.   Visa & Master Charge   456-3756

---

deBALL GIRMES FACTORY OUTLET — J. L. de BALL GIRMES OF AMERICA. *Hwy. 74, Old Charlotte Highway. Follow signs. Mon.-Sat. 298-7976.* Velvets for apparel, elegant upholstery, drapes and other uses. Dozens of colors and textures in bolts on display. Cotton-rayon-acrylics. First quality and off standards. 60% savings. Known world wide. Mastercharge. From I-240, exit U.S. 74.

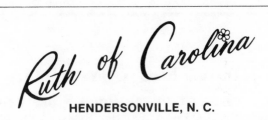

HENDERSONVILLE, N. C.

RUTH OF CAROLINA FACTORY OUTLET. *Located at I-26 and US 64 East.* Open Mon.-Sat. 10-7; Sunday 1-6. (704) 692-3689. A "Best Dressed" list for little girls would surely include children dressed in Ruth of Carolina designs. Ruth Combs has been a pacesetter for 30 years and her creations are sold in leading stores nationally. At the elegant Daisy B. Sample Plant, you can outfit your favorite child for a fraction. Daytime dresses, sports coordinates, and lovely long dresses for special occasions. Toddler 2 to size 14 for girls. Tremendous savings on quality fabric, trim, lace and appliques used on Ruth's designs. These are great for the home seamstress.

Ruth of Carolina now has a French Connection! The company has recently joined forces with Paron S.A. of Troyes, France, one of the oldest and largest manufacturers of children's clothes in Europe. The French label is Absorba, U.S.A. Make this shop a must! Stop by and purchase quality dresses, designer jeans, sweaters, blouses and Absorba products.

THE *WORLD of CLOTHING*

THE WORLD OF CLOTHING. *US 64 East at I-26, Hendersonville, N. C.* Open 7 days a week, 8 am-11 pm. Plan to spend the day here, this is **The Family Outlet.** Not only will you find every top name brand imaginable (at savings of 33% to 75% below retail), under the 75,000 square foot roof, but there is also a TV room and a snack bar! Clothe everyone from infants to grandparents at "the biggest outlet in the world under one roof." Locally owned and operated; highly recommended. Don't miss it.

♥HIPMAN'S
FACTORY OUTLET

CHIPMAN'S. *Two locations: East Flat Rock, N. C. Take US 176 exit from I-26; also in Asheville on Coxe Avenue, under the Hadley Outlet.* An old favorite in bargain shopping for the family. Apparel for men, women and children including such well-known names as Ship 'n Shore, Lee, Maverick, Koret Hang Ten, Lily of France and Hanes. Stockings by famous manufacturers for large department stores. Open all year, Mon.-Sat.

YOUNG GENERATIONS FACTORY OUTLET. *Fourth Ave. East at Grove Street, Hendersonville, N. C. 28739.* Mon.-Sat. 10 am-5 pm. (704) 693-8625. Sportswear and dresses for girls, sizes 7-14 and young junior. These good-looking garments are sold nationally through better department and specialty stores under the tradename PICTURE ME. First quality and irregulars available at significant discounts. Store is in an old factory with plenty of parking.

HOUSE OF TOWELS. *1971 Asheville Highway (US 25), Hendersonville, N.C. (704) 692-9553.* Complete home decorating center. Special prices in bed and bath furnishings from top manufacturers- Wamsutta, Cannon, Fieldcrest, Martex. Fashion colors and patterns in towels, sheets, dust ruffles, spreads and comforters. Table and kitchen linens. A shop that keeps expanding with pretty things.

COLONY CASUALS. *NC 191 North. 692-4336.* An old favorite, this is an outlet for a leading sports line. Marvelous bargains in ski wear-jackets and pants in winter season and great sports clothes in the summer. Savings up to 50%. Get on the mailing list to know about ski wear promotions.

BOONE-BLOWING ROCK AREA

iron⊕mountain
LAUREL BLOOMERY, TENNESSEE 37680

IRON MOUNTAIN STONEWARE. *Laurel Bloomery, Tenn. Located between Mountain City, Tenn. and Damascus, Virginia on Tenn. 91. (615) 727-8888.* Retail store open every day except Christmas. Handmade, durable Iron Mountain Stoneware is produced to be used in the freezer, in the oven and under the broiler. Handsome on the table, cups, bowls, saucers, plates and serving pieces have rich, lustrous colors and are great for special gifts or for adding to a collection. Other locations: Country House Village, NC 105, between Linville and Boone (704) 963-5855. Station House, U.S. 321, Blowing Rock, NC (704) 295-3522.

OUTLETS DOWN THE MOUNTAIN – GREENVILLE, S. C.

"JUST KIDS" HER MAJESTY MILL END STORE, *Mauldin, SC. Mauldin exit from I-85. Plant on US 276 at Hwy. 417. (803) 288-2642.* Children's clothes found in top department stores. Her Majesty

slips, panties, sleepwear, dresses and sportswear for girls, sizes infant through 14. Also all major brands of children's clothes including boys sizes infant through 16. Open Mon.-Sat., 10 A.M.-5:30 P.M. all year, except Thanksgiving and Christmas. Other locations: Columbia, SC, Macon, GA, Augusta, GA, Murfreesboro, TN.
Knoxville, TN. Outlets, Ltd. Mall. Lovell Rd. Exit from I-40-I-75

BURLINGTON, N. C. -

THE "OUTLET CAPITAL OF THE SOUTH"

Burlington, with its many excellent textile mills, has been known for years for its local factory outlet stores. Recently, however, Burlington has enjoyed a veritable boom in the number of well-known national manufacturers with outlet stores located here. With new stores opening each week, Burlington has christened itself the "Outlet Capital of the South."

The Holiday Inn of Burlington, with its unique Outlet Information Center, is a necessary stop for the outlet shopper. Here are merchandise displays, free maps and brochures to guide you to the stores selling men's, women's, and children's clothing, fabrics, yarns, leather goods, towels, blankets, sheets, carpet, furniture, and other merchandise at discount prices. In all the outlet shops, you will find the same name brand and quality merchandise that is offered by specialty and department stores throughout the country.

BURLINGTON SHOE OUTLET

BURLINGTON SHOE OUTLET. *I-85 at the Hwy. 49 North Exit, Burlington, N.C. (919) 227-2010.* Mon.-Sat. 9-6, Sunday 1-5. Its hard to believe this beautiful store is an outlet! Located in Burlington's newest outlet complex, this store offers discounts up to 60% on famous brands we all know and trust: Etienne Aigner, Cobbies, Amalfi, Red Cross, Mushrooms, Bass, Easy Street, Nike, Cover Girl and many others. Special "Thursday Room" with savings up to 80% off retail. All shoes are first quality; handbags and accessories are also available.

GASTONIA, N.C.

LUXURY FABRICS AND CRAFTS, *2430 N. Chester St., Gastonia, NC. I-85 and U.S. 321 North. 867-5313.* Bolts of fine drapery and upholstery fabric, trim and lining. One stop shopping for home decorating.

FURNITURE AT DISCOUNT

STYLE CRAFT INTERIORS, Chapel Hill Blvd. (15-501) Durham, N. C. 27707 (919-489-9191) *Finest Furniture; Karastan Carpets.*
THE COUNTRY SHOP, *739 Lenoir Rd. N.W. off US 321, Hickory, NC (704) 322-5010.* Quality furniture in room settings.
BLACKWELDER'S FURNITURE, *US 21 North, Statesville, NC (704) 872-7673*
GRINDSTAFF'S INTERIORS FURNITURE, *927 W. Main St., Forest City, NC (704) 245-4263*
HUNT GALLERIES, INC. *Hwy. 127 N., Hickory, NC (704) 322-4145.* Manufacturer selling direct.
STEVENS FURNITURE CO. *1258 Hickory Blvd., S.W., Lenoir, NC (704) 728-9234 (US 321 South)*

MARION, N.C.

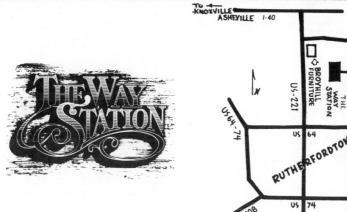

TANNER-THE WAY STATION. *Oak Springs Rd., Rutherfordton, N. C. (704) 287-3637.* "Let's go to Tanner" has always been a favorite invitation for a perfect day-trip. Huge retail shop in rustic building expanded to include shops and a restaurant all known as THE WAY STATION. Part of the Retail Group of Tanner Companies, Inc., The Way Station encompasses the **Doncaster, Tanner Fabric Shop, Men's Shop, Gift Shop, Soup Bowl,** and the **Showroom** (generally known as **The Tanner Dress Shop.**) The showroom features dresses and sportswear-Tanner, Doncaster, Young Traditions. There is also women's apparel from other nationally known brands. Sizes 6-20 in dresses; 4-18 in sportswear. Seconds, samples and first quality overruns. Swimwear and tenniswear in summer. Discounts range from 25% to 70% off regular retail. *Location is ¾ mile north of intersection U.S. 64 and 74 By-pass and one mile east of U.S. 221. Hours 9 to 5 P.M. Mon-Sat.* No charge cards, but checks accepted. Other women's apparel shops: Franklin, Blowing Rock in North Carolina, Pigeon Forge, Tenn., Macon, Ga., Williamsburg Va., Columbia, S. C.,Hilton Head Island, S. C., Myrtle Beach, S.C., Utica N.Y., Norwalk Ct., North Hampton, NH and Rutland, VT.